THE ASHLAND
TRAGEDY

THE ASHLAND
TRAGEDY

Murder, a Mob & a Militia in Kentucky

H.E. "Joe" Castle & J.M. Huff

Published by The History Press
Charleston, SC
www.historypress.com

Copyright © 2021 by H.E. Castle
All rights reserved

Adapted from *The Ashland Tragedy; The Crow-bar and the Ax—The Silent Witnesses*, originally published circa 1885 by James M. Huff.

First published 2021

Manufactured in the United States

ISBN 9781467146647

Library of Congress Control Number: 2020944175

Notice: The information in this book is true and complete to the best of our knowledge. It is offered without guarantee on the part of the authors or The History Press. The authors and The History Press disclaim all liability in connection with the use of this book.

All rights reserved. No part of this book may be reproduced or transmitted in any form whatsoever without prior written permission from the publisher except in the case of brief quotations embodied in critical articles and reviews.

CONTENTS

Preface 7

1. Introduction 9
2. The Fire 15
3. The Search 20
4. Gibbons Found 28
5. A Confession 32
6. The River Chase 38
7. Neal's Trial 47
8. Craft's Trial 68
9. Burnett's Theory 73
10. George Ellis 82
11. New Trials 90
12. River Massacre 96
13. Resolve and Recovery 104
14. Ellis Craft 110
15. William Neal 122
16. Commentary 126

Brief Biographies 133
Pictures 139
Notes 143
About the Authors 155

PREFACE

In this age of general knowledge, where newspapers do not allow details of a murder to escape their columns, we become accustomed to the startling headlines that tell of rape, murder and other horrible crimes. The motives for committing crimes are various. Judge, jury and the public are influenced by the circumstances under which a crime is committed—extenuating causes are carefully considered. The sympathy of a community may be aroused in behalf of a man who has not only murdered but maimed and mangled his victim in the most horrible manner, if a cause is assigned that touches the hearts of the people. Americans are inclined to forgiveness, and the cell of a convicted murderer is often fragrant with roses plucked by the hand of some fair belle, who would cry out with horror at the mere thought of the crime.

In this book is the written history of a crime without extenuating circumstances, so hideous that in all the annals of black deeds it would be difficult to find its parallel.

The authors, in submitting this book to the public, can but feel that they are answering the (silent or expressed) wishes of all who have heard of this remarkable case. And possessing a knowledge of it in all its details, given in a concise, readable form the whole history without reservation, we feel that a plain statement of the facts will not only be read and appreciated, but will contain a lesson so full of warning, so full of unspoken advice, that some who are inclined to violate the law may be checked and brought to consider the awful result. We do not offer you pen pictures drawn from

Preface

a vivid imagination, but truths—plain and unvarnished. Having been present at the fire and looked upon the charred remains of the murdered ones, as a natural consequence, we became interested to know how and by whom this terrible crime had been committed. And from that morning on through the days of excitement and suspense, we watched the chain of evidence as it grew.[1]

As the crime's unthinkable and chaotic aftermath ensued, we noticed with utter disappointment how the subterfuge of a political machine crippled the wheels of justice and wronged the people of Ashland until even greater atrocities were accomplished.

And we fancy that in this truth our readers will find a story of such interest that to enlarge upon it would be gross injustice to all who wish to know about this dark period of history.[2]

1
INTRODUCTION

After breakfast, Deputy Armstrong delivered the new suit of clothes sent to Ellis Craft from his mother. "I slept sound last night," Craft said. "I never woke till the sun came in at the window. I haven't seen the sun rise for many a day, and I asked them to awake me that I might take my last look at it. I have given up all hope. In a few hours I will be a dead man. You are going to hang an innocent man."[3]

At 12:34 p.m. on October 12, 1883, Ellis Craft was taken from the jail to the street, where a buggy waited to carry him to the gallows. A guard of armed men surrounded the buggy as it passed through teeming streets and houses filled with eager spectators. A crowd of more than five thousand men, women and children assembled round about the scaffold to witness the first public hanging in Carter County, Kentucky. Accompanied by Sheriff Holcomb and his deputies, Craft was greeted by Reverend J.P. Pinkerton as he ascended the platform.[4]

The pine scaffold had been framed in a hollow surrounded by hills, allowing unobstructed views for the large gathering. A low-lying blanket of dark gray clouds releasing a drizzling rain would have made a better backdrop for the day's dreary event. Instead, the sun shone brightly and warmth filled the air, providing the setting with an autumn carnival–like atmosphere.

It is here, many folks thought, and even hoped, an admission of guilt would spring forth. The gallows have yielded many eleventh-hour confessions, and it was widely known Craft had staunchly maintained his innocence from the very beginning of this renowned ordeal.

This was a day many thought might never come, for though Craft had been convicted twice of the terrible crime, he had managed to capture for himself a great deal of conjectured support. Some, once certain of Craft's guilt, now weren't altogether convinced Craft had anything to do with the murders. During his lengthy incarceration at Lexington, Craft had routinely received visits from thousands of admirers and enough favorable press to elevate his status to that of a cultic celebrity. Therefore, a confession today would remove all doubt and clear the minds of any misgivings over his hanging. Horses were muzzled and children hushed as Craft began to speak.

> *Dear friends you all know why I'm here and I know that all of you have wished to hear what I have to say. I have been charged with a crime for which I am innocent. Now you all know this is not the time or place to tell a lie. I've said before and I say again, you might as well hang a newborn babe for I am as innocent of this crime as the babe. I was not at the Gibbons' house the night that awful crime was committed. Would that I was, for if I were those precious girls would be alive today. I loved those children dearly and would never have thought to harm a hair on their heads. And now as I am about to swing between the heavens and the earth, I'll tell you what I think caused my death. False witnesses and men like Mr. Heflin, Mr. Campbell and Mr. Russell have desired to see me hang. But I believe that one day God, in His great power and mercy, will see to it that the guilty one will be hung.*[5]

The previous morning, Craft, under heavy guard, was taken to the Little Sandy River on the outskirts of Grayson and baptized again, this time by Reverend Pinkerton. The reverend said he'd talked to dying men before, but he'd never met a man such as Craft. He said Craft showed no remorse and bitterly accused wealthy men of setting him up merely for the reward. He also said Craft seemed strikingly calm for a man in his predicament. He talked at length about his friends and family. Then he asked the reverend to write a letter to his mother and father to inform them that he died innocent and in peace.[6]

Later on that same day, Craft received an encouraging letter from Detective Alf Burnett, who claimed to have found the true guilty parties and protested Craft's innocence to Governor J. Proctor Knott. In the letter, Burnett claimed to make an arrest soon, and he begged the governor for a respite on Craft's behalf. This letter, along with other letters Craft had received, afforded the condemned the hope his neck might be saved before the trap door would be sprung.[7]

Ellis Craft entered his twenty-ninth year on this earth [in July of this year, 1883], and as he stood on the scaffold, he surveyed the large crowd through small, dark eyes that did not disclose the look of a killer. But then seldom ever does a face betray the wicked thoughts or the devilish bent of one's character. The son of a Baptist preacher, Craft was raised in the light of the good book, yet he had gained for himself the reputation of a scamp and a hooligan, being described as a man of inordinate animal passions who would go to unusual lengths to gratify them. His past was peppered with philandering and misdemeanors.[8]

The sober-minded thinker understands reputation alone does not make one a murderer, but it is difficult for even the best of jurors to disavow what is loosely known. And moreover, the people's court of public opinion ever hastens to condemn those of sullied reputations. Despite that, Craft possessed a brash coolness and coarse charisma that—more often than not—worked in his favor. Up until now, he had always leaned on his persuasive powers and silver tongue to wriggle out of any serious trouble. Though he was adept at flowery speech, Craft's words always carried more volume than substance. And now, even with death staring him in the face, he relished his captive audience. Any other time the authorities might have stopped him short, but given the circumstances, he was obliged to speak on.[9]

> *I'd like to thank Mr. Tyree for showing kindness to me while I've been in his jail, and all of the good people of Carter County for their kindness. I only wish I had the opportunity to repay you with more than just words. Folks, I know it's too late for me, but friends don't forget poor brother Neal. For if justice was done, he'd never been separated from his dear wife and their little children. And if justice was done, I'd still be home with my mother and father. I call upon all you mothers and fathers to teach your children right from wrong like my dear mother and father did for me. I have a good father and mother who raised me right. I stand here before all of you and my God and declare that I am innocent of murdering those children. And I hope the Gibbonses and Thomases can find a way to forgive me for something that others have done.*[10]

As he completed his speech, Craft broke into song and sang a hymn:

Did Christ o'er sinners weep,
And shall our cheeks be dry?
Let floods of penitential grief
Burst forth from every eye.

The Son of God in tears
The wondering angels see:
Be thou astonished, O my soul;
He shed those tears for thee.[11]

 Incredibly, Craft maintained his composure despite the somber and piteous occasion. Among the spectators, many cheeks became dampened with tears, especially those of Craft's family and friends. Others were naturally saddened by the solemn event. Craft had maintained a cool appearance since the day the jury sentenced him to hang, and it had been his calm demeanor and flamboyance that had since caused some to doubt his guilt. For those who believed the jury rightly convicted him, justice was but a few moments away.
 As he paused with his head bowed, the multitude stood silent, supposing Craft to be praying. Having tarried longer than what he considered necessary, Reverend Pinkerton stepped forward to speak—all at once, Craft raised his head toward heaven and continued singing:

He wept that we might weep;
Each sin demands a tear;
In Heaven alone no sin is found,
And there's no weeping there.

 The crime that had brought Ellis Craft to the gallows was committed nearly two years previous, in neighboring Boyd County, at the outskirts of the industrious city of Ashland. Geiger's Addition to Ashland, Geigersville and East Ashland all refer to that same community in which this most horrible crime took place. The news of this crime captivated the entire nation, and were it not for the trial of a demented lawyer-turned-assassin named Charles Guiteau who shot President Garfield, this crime and its aftermath would have received more national notoriety than any other during its time. The *Cincinnati Enquirer* described it as "one of the most atrocious and hellish murders ever committed in a civilized community."[12]
 The *Atlanta Constitution* called it a terrible tale of inhuman depravity and "the greatest criminal sensation that ever occurred in this section."[13]
 The *Portsmouth Times* read: "In all the annals of crime there certainly is chronicled no more horrible deed of utter heartlessness, of fiendish brutality and total depravity than this."[14]
 The *Ironton Register* had this to say about it: "Never did a tragedy, in all this region, arouse such indignation as the murder of those innocent children.

Every phase of the story was revolting and every feature of the bloody deed most inhuman."[15]

Ashland, Kentucky, is situated on the Ohio River 15 miles above Huntington, West Virginia, and 130 miles below Cincinnati, Ohio. The city was laid out by engineer Martin T. Hilton and named in 1854 by Levi Hampton, a close friend of the Great Compromiser, Henry Clay.[16] Hampton proposed to rename the settlement, heretofore known as Poage Settlement, after Henry Clay's Lexington, Kentucky farm—Ashland.[17]

Although they were natives of Scotland, the Poages came to colonial America from Ireland in the early eighteenth century, and soon after the Revolutionary War, they left Virginia for Kentucky. As the soil was rich in iron ore deposits, the pig-iron industry began to flourish and several furnaces sprang up. By 1875, seventy-nine charcoal furnaces had been built and placed in operation, and the area soon became one of the country's leading producers of iron.[18]

The first locomotive, the *Constitution*, arrived in Ashland in 1856, and the railroad boosted the city's progress and prosperity at a remarkable rate.[19] As the farming and iron industries increased, so did the population. Schools, churches and hotels were constructed to nurture the intellectual, spiritual and social needs of the citizens, who would be described in 1857 by Sophia Poage Payne in a letter to her son as "a social religious sort of folks."[20]

Industry and growth in Ashland slowed a bit during the Civil War, but the effect was not drastic. In a state divided like no other, Northeastern Kentucky, which included Ashland and Boyd County, remained overwhelmingly loyal to the Union. The citizens collaborated to form their own Ashland Home Guards to protect their families, homes and neighbors from any would-be guerrilla raiders.[21]

And in comparison, Ashland braved the war with only moderate difficulty. The people of Ashland had grown to work and worship, fraternize and fight, if need be, as a unified and well-disposed assembly. The local farmers knew how to work the land and make it bountiful. The industry leaders were enterprising as well as knowledgeable. Religious leaders were strong men of faith. The city's government was composed of honest and hardworking men. All the ingredients were in place for the inhabitants of Ashland to enjoy happy, prosperous and safe lives. The people of Ashland and those who would come to live there were a like-minded lot who shared the same philosophies of life: work hard, live right and enjoy the fruits of labor. Unlike many of the towns that popped up along the Ohio River, Ashland failed to follow the rowdy river town blueprint. There was no time or tolerance for miscreants and scoundrels. The need for a jail didn't arise until five years after the city was laid out, and that was prompted only by the passing of an ordinance stating that all hogs running loose on the streets would be arrested. Meandering hogs tracking mud through the stores was bad for business.[22]

The town progressed, and the people prospered harmoniously. Eventually, the jail would house more than just hogs and minor offenders, yet for the most part, the city's collective voice of justice kept lawlessness in check. And as added security, a town marshal was elected along with district constables.

By all accounts, the manner in which this town developed seems as if it were constructed by divine design. But nothing could have prepared its people for what was about to thrust them into a national spotlight of horror. For on Christmas Eve 1881, a sinister wind would blow through the outskirts of Ashland and enlarge upon itself until it had encompassed the entire city in a cyclone of unthinkable evil.

2
THE FIRE

The five o'clock whistle at the Norton Iron Works indicated the end of work for the day shift. On this Friday, December 23, 1881, however, it also signaled the beginning of the Christmas holiday. Christmas was just two days away and whatever preparations were left would be made with the usual frantic, yet joyful efforts. And this is where our story begins.

The Christmas season traditionally brings out the best in people. For a time, once a year, hustling and hoarding are discarded in favor of sharing and giving, even for those who aren't accustomed to such graces. Merry hearts and well-wishers abound during that time of the year when even the most callous of men give way to some form of benevolence. For some, the Christmas season brings fanciful feasts and festive get-togethers, while for others it brings special gifts and unabated reverence for the Almighty's tender mercy. For Martha Gibbons, however, this Christmas was to bring the unexpected trepidation of every mother's worst fear.

Martha lived in that part of Ashland known as Geiger's Addition, or East Ashland, with her husband, John, and three of their youngest children. They lived in a small one-and-a-half-story dwelling partly owned by a local merchant, C.C. Geiger.[23]

Eleven-year-old Sterling Gibbons was the youngest of those three children. Having turned fourteen on the twenty-second of the previous month, Fannie Gibbons was a pretty girl who had matured early and was well-liked by all who knew her. Seventeen-year-old Robert "Robbie" Gibbons was an industrious young lad whose work as a nail-feeder at the Norton Iron Works provided most of the income for the impoverished family. Much admiration for Robbie was held by all those who knew him, particularly the men who worked with him at the Norton Iron Works, mostly because everything he did, he did with only one leg. Ten years earlier, when Robbie was seven years old, a railcar accident resulted in one of his legs being severed just below the knee. Pity for Robbie grew into admiration, as he never seemed to let it bother him much, and he always remained upbeat regardless of his handicap. He had learned to get around very well with his crutch, and when confronted by those who felt sorrow for him, he quickly reminded them that his future was bright, for he looked forward to the day when, in Heaven, he would once again have both legs.[24]

Martha Gibbons had grown up in that part of Virginia that would become West Virginia, where her father, Joseph Rhodes, had settled to farm a small parcel of land after migrating there from Europe. As she embarked on womanhood, Martha was eager to begin her own life and start a family of her own. The man who would oblige her desire was John Gibbons. Twenty years her senior, John Gibbons came to town and literally swept Martha off her feet in a whirlwind courtship. It was a courtship that was not well received by Martha's family, particularly her father. Very little was known about this man, Gibbons, and the vast age difference left most wondering if Martha had taken leave of her senses. But Martha was anxious for marriage and eager to start a family of her own. John Gibbons said all the right things, and he seemed to have a little money, so Martha answered his proposal with an exuberant yes.[25]

Theirs was a marriage, however, that would be marked by few ups and considerable downs. Shortly after the marriage, the couple located in Point Pleasant, West Virginia, where they found favor among the people. And in a short time, John Gibbons was elected their town marshal. Things were going well, and John, a carpenter by trade, was awarded a contract to build a new county jail. The couple began to prosper, and they started a family, but as the new jail was near completion, it caught fire and burned. Distraught by the misfortune, the couple ventured west and landed in Missouri, where John's work soon afforded them a small parcel of land. The family continued to grow, and again they prospered. Interrupted by service in the Civil War, John returned home to a feeling of resentment by finding his land had been confiscated. John brought his family back to West Virginia for a while but soon moved and settled in Ashland, Kentucky. Some folks found Gibbons to be a likeable fellow, and shortly after moving to Ashland, he was urged to run for mayor and nearly won.[26]

On that fateful December 23 Friday afternoon, Martha Gibbons and young Sterling left their house and boarded a buggy on their way to Ironton, Ohio, to stay the night with Kate Shore, one of Martha's married daughters. She had planned to make a few small purchases (probably Christmas gifts) at the general store in Ironton the next day and then return home later that Christmas Eve.[27]

From the buggy, Martha hailed neighbor, Caroline Thomas, and asked if she would allow her daughter Emma to stay the night with Fannie and Robert since she'd be away for the night. Thomas agreed and assured Martha she would have Emma stay with Fannie and Robert. That little arrangement would have been unnecessary if John Gibbons had been home, but he had left Ashland a few days before Thanksgiving and his whereabouts were currently unknown. Emma wasn't necessarily asked to babysit for her neighbors as much as simply to provide company for Fannie until, and after, Robbie returned home from work somewhere around 8:30 p.m. Emma Carico was Caroline Thomas's daughter by her first marriage. The widow had since remarried Harrison Thomas, which is why her daughter Emma is sometimes known as Emma Carico and other times known as Emma Thomas. Emma, a young girl like Fannie Gibbons, had also matured early for her age. Her presence at the house with Fannie and Robert provided Martha Gibbons with a certain measure of comfort.[28]

Fannie and Emma were not only neighbors but also best friends. And although the two girls were excited about the Christmas holiday, they also shared in another type of excitement that was typical of girls their age. They had both embarked upon the age when the talk of boys and dating was predominant in their conversation. Fannie had turned fourteen a month ago, and Emma would have been fourteen on the next Wednesday, December 28.[29]

Shortly after 6:00 p.m., Emma said goodbye to her mother and went next door to the Gibbons house, where Fannie was waiting for her. Newspaper editor J.M. Huff provides the details about why this was the last time Caroline Thomas saw her daughter alive.

The next morning, Thomas arose about 4:30 a.m. and instinctively looked out the window toward the Gibbons house. Seeing nothing, she stoked the fire and went outside to bring in some more wood. After replenishing the fire, she glanced once again through the window toward the Gibbons house and saw what looked to be a lamp burning in the front room window. Thinking it to be too early for the kids to be out of bed, she stepped outside to get a better look when she realized it was not a lamp she saw but flames coming out of the window. Immediately, she ran toward the house screaming, "Fire!" As she got closer, she could see the fire was spreading and knocked on the front door while screaming for Emma. She tried to open the door to no avail. It was locked.

She ran around to the side door as she continued to yell, "Fire!" The side door was unlocked, and she was able to enter the house, but the smoke was so thick she could advance no further. She yelled for Emma and the others but got no response. As the smoke from the room forced her back out onto the porch, she ran shrieking, "Fire!" as some of the neighbors began to arrive. Joseph Arthur was the first on the scene, followed quickly by George Faulkner, John W. House, John Mead and others. All this occurred in less time, perhaps, than it has taken to read the account of it. Very soon, enough people had rushed to the scene to form a bucket brigade, but the partially frozen ground made it difficult to gather much water from the tiny stream that flowed beside the house. Meanwhile, the frantic Thomas was soon able to get George Faulkner to understand that her daughter, Emma, was inside the house along with the Gibbons children. Thomas was becoming delirious and had to be restrained lest she impede the vigorous rescue efforts.

Faulkner broke in one of the windows on the upper side of the house, reached in and felt in on the lounge where he knew Robbie Gibbons usually slept, but found he was not there. He then went around to the lower side window next to where the girls slept, breaking the same in with an ax. And through the flickering flames and the oscillating smoke his first glance fell upon a hand as though protruding from a body prostrate on the floor. The sight was awful, and he turned away, sickened. J.W. House then reached in and caught hold of the arm, pulling the body toward the window, making an effort to lift it out, but could not. He called for help and was assisted by a Black neighbor, and together they succeeded in lifting what afterward proved to be the corpse of Emma Carico, terribly burned and disfigured.

J.W. House afterward went into the house, and in the smoke and flames, he searched around for the other bodies. On the bed, covered with burning bedclothes, he found Fannie Gibbons and, catching her up, took her out at the lower side window. After catching a quick breath of air, he reentered the burning structure. Almost maddened by the choking, blinding smoke and quickened by the crackling, hissing flames, he stumbled upon an oilcan on the floor, near the sewing machine. Then he found Robbie, who was lying with his head under the stairs. He dragged him out onto the little side porch and was helped by Cyrus Wilson in carrying the body away.

By this time, a large crowd had gathered, and many of the respondents were fighting the fire, while others were trying to save some of the Gibbonses' humble belongings. More belongings might have been saved were it not for some confusion about whether little Sterling Gibbons was in the house. By the time it was realized he was not inside, the fire had gained such headway that very little could be done to stop it.

The bodies of the three children were laid out on some smoke-infused bedsheets that had been taken out of the house. As the charred and disfigured bodies of the innocent children lay cold on the ground, those in attendance were sickened by the horrible sight and the stench of burned flesh. Caroline Thomas was inconsolable.

The morning light began to spread over the scene, and the bodies were laid out on a mattress and covered with bedclothes. The hurry and excitement of the fire gave place to a feeling of commiseration and pity for those who had, as was then supposed, burned and suffocated in the house. People of all ages, White and Black, male and female rushed to the site upon hearing the terrifying news, but they could not bear to gaze upon the heart-sickening sight of the charred and disfigured bodies of the innocents, who had just a few hours before teemed with joy and hope. But the morning light, the enemy of evil, revealed a story of such fearful significance that faces blanched, and strong men lost their nerve. The children had been murdered! The dread intelligence started in a whisper, and as it passed from mouth to mouth, it grew in volume until a perfect storm of indignant fury was aroused. Who were the perpetrators of this awful crime? Who could answer?[30]

3

THE SEARCH

As the feelings of anguish and sorrow transformed into furious concern at the realization of what lay before them, an impromptu search for evidence began. A closer look at the bodies revealed the brain was oozing from a wound in Robbie's head, and the skulls of both the girls were found to be crushed. The bedclothes were examined, and blood was found upon them. Blood was also found on the pillows. Robbie Gibbons was the least burned of the three, but the two girls were burned nearly beyond recognition, particularly in the areas below their midsections. And it was clear the fire on the bed in which the girls had slept had gained more headway than at any other spot in the house.[31]

More evidence of the crime was immediately apparent. An old ax was found under some pieces of smoldering carpet with hair and blood on its battered poll. A crowbar was discovered through a crack in a fence. It was also speckled with blood and clinging hair. These were evidently the instruments used to commit the awful crime, and they almost certainly indicated the presence of more than one perpetrator. It seemed clear that the children were murdered and the house fired in an attempt to cover up the crime.[32]

The bodies of the children were removed to the home of a nearby neighbor, and the news of the fire and the murders spread rapidly. Cries of pity and indignation were heard throughout the city. There was much excitement. Upon notification, Justice of the Peace Thomas Russell hurried to the scene and impaneled a jury to conduct an initial inquest to determine the causes of the deaths. Drs. J.W. Martin, J.H. Wade and W.F. Tiernan were also summoned, and their initial examination produced the following individual reports: ROBERT GIBBONS—The upper part of the left parietal bone was driven in for an area that would square about three inches. Some of the lacerated brains running out. FANNIE GIBBONS—Found entire surface of the body changed. The whole frontal bone was driven back on the brain and squeezing a part of it out of the skull. EMMA THOMAS (CARICO)—The surface of the body burned, the parietal and temporal bones on the left side were driven down on the brain and the irregular shape of the fracture would square an area of about two and a half inches. The examinations revealed enough for all three physicians to believe both girls were raped. The outrage of the populace knew no bounds, and the necessity of pursuing an investigation was immediately wrought to discover and bring the inhuman villains to justice and due punishment.[33]

Brushing all their Christmas plans and festivities aside, the civic leaders quickly called for a meeting, yet another dreadful and sorrowful duty had to be carried out. The awful news had to be taken to Martha Gibbons. Martha had her heart pierced just one year ago when death prematurely stole her youngest, five-year-old Harry, away from her. It has been said that God sheds a special grace on mothers who have lost children so that they may persevere through life after such a heavy loss. Only a mother who has lost a child can truly understand the heartache, the misery and the bitterness that naturally accompanies the loss of a child. But what about two and three? And to have lost them in such a horrible and tragic manner? The fear was real that poor Martha's heart might fail on hearing the frightful news. A company of five volunteered to travel to Ironton that morning to give Martha the terrible news. C.C. Geiger, part owner of the house, and his wife, Margaret, along with Martha's neighbors, the Powells, and Dr. J.D. Tiernan made that mournful trip.

The special meeting convened that Christmas Eve afternoon at 2:00 p.m. in the Aldine Hotel. The meeting was attended by hundreds of people representing all classes. Mayor John Means called the meeting to order. Motion was made and carried to allot a $200 reward for information leading to the arrest and conviction of the perpetrator(s). A committee of six was appointed to solicit money to donate to the families and to pay for detectives to work up the case. A separate committee of three was appointed to oversee the distribution of the money and to hire a detective. A.C. Campbell, cashier of the Ashland National Bank; John Calder, hardware merchant; and John Russell, president of the Norton Iron Works, comprised what would be called the Citizens Committee—three good men.[34]

During times like this, level heads are required. These three men knew they had to act swiftly. The perpetrator(s) must be apprehended and quickly before they could leave the area. The grieving families must be taken care of, and the safety and security of the citizens must be provided. The threat of vigilante justice must be preempted, for there was already some talk of a lynching. And they knew, as was common, the newspapers would stoke the kindled fire of vigilante justice at every opportunity.

> *It does not seem possible that the perpetrators of this fearful crime can long escape detection. It is safe to say that their tenure of life will be very brief after they are caught and returned to Ashland.*
> —Cincinnati Enquirer, *December 25, 1881*

> *Excitement in Ashland and vicinity is at fever height, and if the human devils are captured, they will likely not be accorded the formality and monotonous delay of a jury trial.*
> —Portsmouth Times, *December 31, 1881*

> *From the way in which the people talk it will be a miracle if lynch law doesn't prevail in case the commission of the bloody deed in question be fastened upon anybody in this vicinity.*
> —Cincinnati Enquirer, *December 26, 1881*

The men of the Citizens Committee had their work cut out for them, but they were doing their best to approach the situation with the savvy of experienced crime fighters. They also knew they had to fend off their own feelings of vengeance lest they fall victim themselves to the call of vigilante justice.

Everything connected with the murders was now of deep and absorbing interest; the smallest incident relative to it was rehearsed again and again. The reward was increased by private subscription until it amounted to about $1,000. Some reports had it growing as high as $3,000. The Citizens Committee sent dispatches to several detectives, including Alf Burnett from Charleston, West Virginia, and John T. Norris from Springfield, Ohio. To the displeasure of Burnett, the Committee agreed to hire the more experienced forty-two-year-old Norris, who was widely known and had a reputation for success. His work on the Little Reddy McKimie gang three years back was still on the lips of most everyone familiar with that case.[35]

Regardless, the thirty-one-year-old Burnett, founder and chief detective of the recently incorporated Eureka Detective Agency, showed great interest in the case and traveled to Ashland with the intent of solving the crime and perhaps cashing in on the reward money.[36]

The next morning, Christmas Day, Commonwealth Attorney Stephen G. Kinner and County Coroner James R. Ford arrived on the scene to hold a more thorough postmortem examination of the bodies. A jury was impaneled as another inquest was held. The verdict of this jury was nearly the same as the one given on the previous day.[37]

On Monday morning, the time had come to bury the poor victims. The funeral at the Methodist-Episcopal Church-South was attended by a large crowd of people. Though it had rained all morning, the church was crowded to overflowing. The funeral sermon was preached by the Reverend T.S. Wade, with other ministers taking part in the services. About eighty nail feeders who had worked with Robbie Gibbons walked from the mill to the church. Sadness reigned at the uncommon sight of three coffins in the church. Despite the inclement weather, the largest funeral procession ever in this city was witnessed that day. Carriages, buggies and wagons carried many folks, while others walked through the mud from the church to the Ashland Cemetery. The scene at the cemetery was heartrending as the two mothers wept uncontrollably while the remains of the three children were interred in one grave.[38]

The funerals of the three poor children left the citizens with a feeling of immeasurable gloom. A large dose of the darker side of life had invaded their domain and smacked them square in the face, with no apologies. Questions of why and how remained stifled behind quivering lips, and parents looked on their children with haunting thoughts of those three who now rested cold in the ground.

That same morning, Detective Norris arrived in Ashland and went straight to work. He was taken to the scene of the crime, where even the chimney of the small house had come down. He commenced to sift through the rubble as he looked for evidences and clues, while an excited Cincinnati newspaper reporter followed him around like a little puppy eager to note every move made by Norris and any new things worthy of print. Norris spent the better part of the afternoon interviewing neighbors and those who were present at the burning house that morning. After gathering as much information he could, he had an extended conversation with Martha Gibbons. Norris claimed he would hesitate to formulate a theory until he felt sure about the identity of the murderer(s).[39]

After learning that old man Gibbons had been absent from their home for more than a month, he focused his interrogation of Martha on her husband. Largely on the strength of this interview, he discovered enough about the old man that by 9:00 p.m. that night, he believed he had solved the crime and the guilty party was none other than John Gibbons. He believed that their ongoing family disputes and problems had finally led the old man to act on previous threats of domestic violence. His theory had John Gibbons returning to Ashland under the cover of darkness that night to kill his family and subsequently killing himself. Norris said Gibbons must have mistaken Emma Carico for his own wife, Martha. His theory was supported by a letter Martha had received from her husband eleven years earlier that read as follows:

> *When old men have outlived all their friends it is then time for them to die. I have no idea of ever committing the rash act of self-destruction. If I do, it will be where you and the children will never see me. I feel as if I had not a friend on earth, and is it reasonable that I should want to live any longer? Others have put an end to their existence; how, then can you expect me to live and witness my own shame? I have struggled fifty-seven years alone in the world, and I find my life has been a blank. All my efforts have been a failure. My whole life has been spent in running after baubles that always burst when I touched them.*[40]

Detective Norris also thought that old man Gibbons was the only one who would have known the locations of the ax, the crowbar and the oilcan that was used to fire the house. Norris showed a great measure of confidence in his theory. And that inspired others to also believe who might have otherwise doubted. He sent out cards all over the surrounding country describing Gibbons as sixty-eight years old, five feet, nine inches tall and weighing about 140 pounds. He believed that if Gibbons had already done himself in, his body could probably be found either in a nearby pond or in the Ohio River. A reward was offered for the body.[41]

The *Cincinnati Enquirer* immediately took up the cry and sent the news to thousands of subscribers that old man Gibbons was the guilty wretch who murdered his own children. The *Enquirer* and other newspapers did not hesitate to paint John Gibbons as a vile, contemptible and devilish beast. Gibbons was portrayed as a shiftless ne'er-do-well who ran from his troubles rather than face them. His reckless living left him and his family nearly destitute much of the time. It was said that early in the marriage, Gibbons had borrowed money from his brother-in-law and never paid it back. While living in Point Pleasant, West Virginia, Gibbons, a carpenter by trade, got a contract to build a new county jail. It was said he took out an insurance policy on the building and then hired a man to burn it while he collected the insurance on it and ran off with the money out west to Missouri. While there, it was reported that he joined ranks with the Confederate army when the Civil War broke out, but he deserted and moved back to Kanawha County, West Virginia. He very often grew despondent and listless and allowed his wife and young daughters to do most of the work that provided for the family.[42]

It was also reported that Gibbons had a daughter from a previous marriage and the death of his first wife was shrouded in mystery. And the word was that on one occasion the old man had asked Martha to enter into a suicide pact with him; he frequently abused her, and the children were afraid of him due to his violent temper. In addition, and according to the conversation Detective Norris had with Martha Gibbons, the old man had frequently threatened to burn the house and kill his family. Martha told the detective that for years she had feared he might do something like that. By virtue of these printed exposés, John W. Gibbons had quickly become one of the most hated and hunted men in America.[43]

Many of the local citizens took up the cause and conducted their own investigations. Some of the folks were anxious to find either the old man or perhaps anyone else who might have been connected to the crime, for justice's sake. Others became busy searching just for the reward money. Several folks were detained or arrested on suspicion, and many theories were developed, but Detective Norris, after careful examination, exploded them all and remained satisfied about his own theory that named John Gibbons as the lone guilty party. The interest in the case continued to grow daily.[44]

Vague rumor said the night of the murders a man was seen to land just above the town and leave his boat, and before the morning light had dawned, he returned and silently floated away. Norris said it was probably old man Gibbons and that he was now, most likely, food for the fishes. Local constable B.R. Pennybacker was employed by Norris to go to West Virginia to search for traces of Gibbons's whereabouts. He returned with the information that a man answering to the description of Gibbons had gotten a skiff (a small rowboat) on the Kanawha River, below Charleston, a day or two before the murder. This event and the mysterious boatman at Ashland were coupled together. A man was found who said he had seen Gibbons at Gallipolis, Ohio, a few days before, and Norris was jubilant. It was known that Gibbons was an avid reader of newspapers and would read every newspaper within reach. His disappearance and continued absence from Ashland then provided more alleged proof that Norris was on the right track and Gibbons was surely the guilty party.⁴⁵

Detective Norris had gathered a large company of men in his employ to canvass the entire area in search of clues that might lead them to Gibbons or his body. One nearby pond had been dragged in search of Gibbons's body, and another pond near the cemetery was to be dragged the following day. Norris also disagreed with the initial examinations of the girls' bodies and claimed there were no rapes. He said he knew more about this kind of thing than those doctors. This helped to buoy his theory that old man Gibbons was the culprit, and with the help of the excited newspaper correspondents, his theory was gaining ground every day. But not everyone agreed with the detective's theory. Though the three men on the Citizens Committee remained confident in Norris, his brash notion to overrule the doctors on the matter of the rapes led them to wonder whether his self-confidence might have spilled over into rash arrogance. One man who disputed Norris's theory from the very beginning was Deputy U.S. Marshal James Heflin.⁴⁶

The thirty-six-year-old Heflin had been the Maysville, Kentucky town marshal for nine years, and he was also commissioned as a deputy U.S. marshal under Kentucky's U.S. Marshal Robert H. Crittenden. A decorated veteran of the American Civil War, Heflin enlisted in the Union army as an eighteen-year-old private, and in less than a month, he was promoted to sergeant. He was distinguished throughout his time in the military for his gallantry and heroism. As a lawman, Marshal Heflin was acquainted with the criminal element, and his success at ferreting out and bringing to justice lawbreakers of every kind was quite remarkable.⁴⁷ No other lawman in the Ohio Valley was more feared by the worst evildoers of mankind. Just a few months previous, Marshal Heflin had led a company of internal revenue agents into the hills of Letcher County, Kentucky, where they found themselves engaged in a battle with moonshiners who had equipped themselves with a cannon left behind by John Morgan when he raided Kentucky in 1864. After a rather lengthy gun battle, Marshal Heflin's party escaped without injury and escorted five prisoners to Grayson, Kentucky.⁴⁸

Marshal James Heflin arrived in Ashland on Thursday, December 29. What brought him to Ashland? The Citizens Committee had already hired Detective Norris to work up the case. Maybe it was the lure of the reward money. Or perhaps because Marshal Heflin had a thirteen-year-old daughter of his own, he was compelled to come to avenge the deaths of the two innocent girls and the poor boy. He met with the Citizens Committee at the Aldine Hotel and told them he disagreed with Detective Norris's theory naming John Gibbons as the murderer. It was irresponsible and self-serving for Detective Norris to have challenged the doctors' report concerning the two girls. Rape was the most likely motive for the murders. And, if so, it was not possible for Gibbons to have mistaken Emma Carico for his own wife while raping her. And with two obvious weapons used to conclude the foul deeds, it was extremely unlikely the crimes were committed by only one person. There was also a question about the timing of Norris's interrogation of Martha Gibbons. As she was distraught and quite possibly still in a state of shock from learning her two children had met such a terrible fate, doubt remained whether her words should have been considered reliable enough to have pointed an accusing finger.[49]

Marshal Heflin did not think so, and he informed the Citizens Committee he would set out to produce John Gibbons and prove his innocence. He implored the men on the committee to keep his pursuit private. He did not want anyone following him around or getting in his way. He liked to work alone, for that was his style. And without further delay, he started right off in his search for Gibbons. Heflin was taken to the scene of the crimes, where he inspected, probed and searched through the remains of the burned structure. He met with several neighbors and folks who were present at the burning house. He also studied many of the theories brought forward that Detective Norris had previously exploded and found none of them worthwhile to follow. All signs of the missing John Gibbons pointed to West Virginia.[50]

4
GIBBONS FOUND

Marshal Heflin left Ashland on Saturday, December 31, and boarded the train for Huntington, West Virginia. While at the depot in that city, he spoke to Marion Sanford, a man familiar with Gibbons, who told the marshal he saw Gibbons on the day of the murders. From there, Heflin rented a horse and left toward the direction of Hamlin in Lincoln County. The next morning, Sunday, Heflin saw a farmer, Andrew Hager who had come to town to find out about the murders in Ashland. Hager told Marshal Heflin John Gibbons had been working for him and staying at his house for the past two weeks. He explained they had only heard about the murders in Ashland just the previous night since they received the mail but once a week. Gibbons, Hager said, had become very distracted with grief upon hearing that news and wished to go straightway to Ashland. "I begged him to wait," said Hager, "until I could come to town and find out more about it, thinking it could be a mistake."[51]

Upon hearing this from Hager, Heflin lent Hager his rented horse to return to his home and bring Gibbons back with him to Hamlin. After bringing Gibbons up to speed on the intricate details of the case, Marshal Heflin, who knew the state of feeling in Ashland, thought proof would be required to offset the unjust statements of Detective Norris. So, he brought Hager with them, and Hager wrote the following statement:

> *Mr. Gibbons has been at my house since the 19th of December, and since that time until the 1st of January he has not been away from my home for*

more than five hours at a time. I live twenty miles from the nearest railroad depot. I never heard of the murders until Saturday, December 31st; we do not receive but one mail per week. Mr. Gibbons wanted to start right away after we had heard the news, but I persuaded him not to go, and thought it might be someone else. I expected to go to town and find out about it, but he would not remain, and I then let him have a horse, when Mr. Heflin came, and I accompanied them to Ashland.[52]

The three of them arrived in Ashland on Monday morning, January 2, 1882, and in addition to Hager's sworn statement, Marshal Heflin brought the following documents addressed to the Citizens Committee:

Hamlin, Lincoln Co., W.VA.,
Sunday, Jan. 1, 1882.
MESSRS. John Russell, A.C. Campbell, John Calder:

GENTLEMEN—Mr. Heflin is in this place in search of Mr. J.W. Gibbons. Mr. Gibbons is here and will go down with Mr. Heflin, who will be accompanied by Mr. Andrew Hager, who we certify is a man who was raised in this county, and is a man reliable in every respect, a man of truth, and, in fact, known among us as one of our most respectable citizens. He will testify before you as to the time J.W. Gibbons has been here. And we certify that J.W. Gibbons was in this place on Friday, the 23rd of December 1881, and we were in conversation with him up to twelve o'clock of that day. This statement we make and send to you, thinking, as it only contains facts, it may be of assistance or aid to you in fixing the guilt of the terrible crime perpetrated in your city on the guilty man, if he can be found.

This day and date above written.
J.D. Smith, Ex-Justice,
Marion Sanford,
I.V. Sweetland,
John T. Sweetland, Sheriff Lincoln Co., W.Va.
Attest: James Heflin, Deputy U.S. Marshal, Kentucky.

Clerk's Office, County Court of Lincoln County, W.VA.
J.H. Hager, Clerk of Lincoln County Court, do hereby certify that I am well acquainted with J.D. Smith, Marion Sanford, I.V. Sweetland and J.S. Sweetland, citizens of the county of Lincoln, State of West Virginia,

The Ashland Tragedy

all of whom I know to be gentlemen of high standing in this community, and men of veracity and integrity.
Given under my hand and official seal, this 1st day of January 1882.
H. Hager, Clerk, Lincoln County Court, W.Va.[53]

The news that John Gibbons had been found and brought to town spread like wildfire throughout the region. Excitement was aroused to a fever pitch. At 10:00 a.m., a coroner's jury was organized pursuant to adjournment of a week ago. John Gibbons appeared in court. His eleven-year-old son, Sterling, who was with his mother at Ironton on the night of the murders, came in and sat on his father's lap.[54]

Andrew Hager was sworn:

I have lived in Lincoln County, West Virginia for 31 years. Gibbons came to my house Monday, December 19 at 10 o'clock; he stayed there continuously until Sunday night, January 1, 1882, except five hours on Friday, when he borrowed my horse to go to Hamlin, seven miles away, for the mail, and returned at 2 p.m. (His departure from Hamlin at noon is proven in the affidavit given above.) On Friday night there was a large company at my house. Gibbons was present. Our wives are cousins. It is 20 miles from my house to Milton, the nearest railroad station, and 35 miles from there to Ashland. That journey could not be made in less than a day. I first heard of the murder, through a neighbor, Saturday night, December 31. I told Gibbons, who wanted to start for Ashland right off. I persuaded him to wait until the next day, when I would go to Hamlin and verify the report. On my return I met Gibbons a mile from my house, who had become impatient and was coming on foot.[55]

James Heflin, U.S. deputy marshal was sworn:

I went to Huntington, saw Mr. Sanford, who told me that Gibbons was in his town on the day of the murder. I hired a horse and went to Hamlin. I saw Mr. Hager on Sunday, ascertained the facts, and sent my horse out by Mr. Hager for Mr. Gibbons to ride in. When they returned, we three started for Milton, where we took the train at 6 a.m. for this place, arriving at 8 a.m. It would take a younger man and a better rider than Gibbons nine hours to make the journey from Mr. Hager's house to Ashland. I could have brought fifty more witnesses as to Gibbons' whereabouts on Friday, December 23, but thought it unnecessary.[56]

The jury consisted of the following men: A.C. Campbell, C.C. Chinn, William Jordan, G.H. Keener, J.H. Emmons and C.R. Long. They retired and, in a short time, returned a verdict in accordance with the aforementioned facts, exonerating John Gibbons completely.[57]

Detective Norris had left for home the same day Marshal Heflin started for West Virginia, and from his home in Ohio, he telegraphed his congratulations to the insulted father. Congratulations? Congratulations for what? John Gibbons had done nothing worthy of congratulations. Rather than offering congratulations, Norris should have telegraphed an apology. Can any words describe the feelings of John Gibbons, falsely accused of the murder of his own children, hunted, persecuted and slandered? Gibbons's name was not worth much before this ordeal, but thanks in large part to the character assassination by the newspapers and the lousy detective work by John T. Norris, his name had now been smeared to ruins. And could any punishment be too severe for the guilty wretches who could stand calmly by while these accusations were brought forward that might have doomed an innocent man?[58]

After the inquest, Mayor John Means addressed the citizens on behalf of the Citizens Committee.

> *Now that the mystery about Gibbons and his movements have been dissolved, and his innocence established, we must return to the first theory of the crime, which was undoubtedly correct, that the motive was rape, and then murder and arson followed in their efforts at concealment. The criminals are no doubt in our midst, or at least not five miles away, and it is the duty of everyone to be on the alert to assist in discovering them. Let all who have discovered any suspicious conduct, or absence or anything that may lead to a clue, call on anyone of the committee, in confidence, if their information does not lead to any result, the committee will keep the source of their information secret. This crime cannot remain concealed.*[59]

5

A CONFESSION

Not only was the arrival of John Gibbons big news, but the fact Marshal James Heflin was in town, and working on the case, was also on everyone's lips. The citizens held a great amount of confidence in Marshal Heflin, and his presence would likely cause the evildoers, if still in the vicinity, much agitation. Ten days after the terrible crime had been committed, a man named George Ellis, who lived in Geigersville, near the Gibbons house, came to Geiger, Powell & Ferguson's store to buy a cigar. Powell, who was waiting on him, struck up a casual conversation and said, "George, Gibbons has come back, and his skirts are clear of this crime, who is it going to fall on now?"

At this question, Ellis, who had heretofore been perceived as a good, quiet citizen, became noticeably nervous. Powell noticed his hands shaking as he paid for his cigar. After some hesitancy, Ellis said to Powell, "I think I have a clue; and if I had the witnesses it would be all right. But I am afraid they would turn state's evidence."[60]

Powell could not help but notice his odd behavior and asked, "What do you mean by that, George?" Ellis did not answer, and he hurried out of the store. Ferguson, who was present at the store, also noticed George Ellis's erratic behavior and speech.

Ellis then walked to the train depot and was standing at the corner of the building when William H. Eba walked by. Ellis was visibly startled, as if just awakened from a terrible dream. He took Eba by the arm and asked, "Did you want to see me?" Somewhat puzzled, Eba told him that he did not. The word concerning Ellis's strange behavior quickly spread until it was eventually brought to the attention of the Citizens Committee. And for the remainder of the day, Ellis was closely watched, his every movement observed. When the news of Ellis's words and odd behavior reached Marshal Heflin, he had him brought to the Aldine Hotel that evening to tell what he knew to the Citizens Committee. Still showing obvious signs of nervousness, Ellis was slow to tell what he knew and asked very particularly regarding the nature and the effect of turning state's evidence. He was told that anyone guilty of a crime could tell the facts in the case, and whoever was connected with him in the crime, and that the testimony would be taken in court in condemning the others. And sometimes the person telling the facts would be allowed to go free, or, at least, his punishment made lighter.[61]

Ellis fidgeted, stammered and stumbled over his words until he was finally able to speak in a coherent manner. After talking for some time, and saying he believed he could tell who a good witness would be, etc., he commenced and continued almost without interruption until he had narrated the whole story. Strong men—men who would and had faced musket and cannon balls—could not stay in the room while Ellis told of the dreadful deeds committed that night. And as he told of the girls' cries for mercy and how the heartless wretches went on with their work—that would have made devils themselves shrink at the very sight—these men left the room, saying they could not stand to hear it. The following is the confession made by Ellis, written down by A.C. Campbell:

> *While working in the brickyard of Powell & House, William Neal told me that there was a girl in town that he would give five dollars to have intercourse with; Emma Thomas was the girl. "I intend to have intercourse with her if it costs me my life, and that before Christmas." A few nights before Christmas I went home and found Lizzie Church there; afterward came Ellis Craft. Craft said: "I am going to get Fannie Gibbons some black candy and take it to her Christmas Eve night." He said this candy was in all imaginable vulgar shapes. I've heard him say many a time that he was going to have intercourse with Fannie Gibbons before he left the place. He has not been at my house since the murders. I am a good friend of Craft, also a friend of Neal. I give these statements voluntarily, for the good of the community. I assisted at the burning house. I handled the bodies at the fire. I saw both Craft and Neal at the fire early.*
>
> *About midnight, Friday night, Ellis Craft and William Neal came to my gate, called me out, and said: "Come go with us; we are going to*

Gibbons's to have some fun." (Ellis Craft did the talking.) *I refused, when Craft said: "Damn you, you must go," and snapped his revolver at me. I followed them to the Gibbons house. Ellis Craft found an old ax and went to the front window, raised the same, and stepped in; Neal followed, but I stayed behind on the porch. Craft came back to the window and said: "If you don't come in, I will shoot you." I then went in. They opened the inside door, which was near and close to Robbie's bed. Robbie started to get up, when Craft said: "You had better lie still." Craft then went to the bed where the two girls were sleeping and began indecent liberties with them, when Robbie said: "You had better stay away from there," and started to get up, when Craft hit him with the ax. He fell back on the lounge, then made a plunge forward, and fell fully six feet from the bed, under the stairs, where his body was found. The girls screamed. Craft jumped on the bed, when the girls said: "Ellis Craft, what are you here for?" Emma Thomas started to jump out of bed and said: "O! O." Neal then choked her and pulled her off the bed and onto the floor. She fought him, and he called me to help hold her. I held her down by the shoulders while he outraged her. She said: "Oh, Bill, I did not think you would do this," and tried to get up, saying that she would run out and tell her mother. Neal said: "I guess you won't," at the same time striking her on the head with the big end of a crowbar. She threw up her hands as she was struck and died instantly.*

Ellis Craft tried to force Fannie Gibbons. He had some trouble, and said, to me: "Come here and help me!" I only laid my finger on her shoulder, when she lay still—I think she was nearly choked to death. Craft used the ax when he hit Fannie. It was Neal that proposed killing the girls. I said: "Oh, no, boys; don't do that." Neal said: "We had better get away from here." Craft said: "We will be suspected; we had better burn the house." Craft then said to me: "You have got to go hunt some coal oil." I refused, and he said: "I will kill you if you don't." I took the lamp and went into the kitchen and found the can of oil. I returned with it, set the lamp on the sewing machine, and handed the can to Ellis Craft. He refused to take it and said: "You pour the oil on the girls." Fannie was on the bed and Emma was on the floor. I poured the oil all over them, pouring out all the oil in the can on them—a half-gallon can nearly full. Craft and Neal then ordered me to shove the bed around. I did so. Craft struck a match on his pants and set fire to Emma, who was lying on the floor. He then touched a match to Fannie and turned the bed clothing over her. She was lying on the back part of the bed, against the wall.

I then threw down the can and started out and said: "I am going.' One of them said: "If you don't stop till we get ready we will get after you!" I stopped. We were there nearly an hour; but perhaps only half an hour. When we started out the ax was handed me, and I threw it behind the door as I ran out. We all went out the same window through which we entered. Neal carried out the crowbar and threw it down.

We separated at the corner of my lot, and Craft told me: "If you tell this thing we will kill you."'I think they must have returned later and again set fire to the house. I think it was about midnight when we went there; it may have been later. I next saw them at the fire, when Neal said: "That is a bad case."

I tell this because I cannot keep it. I have not slept nor eaten but little since that terrible night. I could not run away. My wife knows nothing of my guilt in this matter. I tell this for fear Craft or Neal will tell it first and turn state's evidence. I want to die, and would have killed myself, but was afraid. All I want is that the guilty parties shall be punished.

My father and mother are living. I have five brothers and three sisters. My wife is a good woman; please take good care of her and send her home before my trouble comes. I would like to see her before I die.

All I ask of this committee is that you pledge your word that you will not let the mob get me before taking me to jail, but take me to prison at once, for I want to get safely in the courthouse, and tell all that happened that terrible night, so that the others may be punished also. I don't want to be hung by the mob until all is told in court. I will trust your pledge to keep me safely till you land me in jail.[62]

By offering this confession, George Ellis freed himself from the heavy burden of his convicted conscience. He realized he was doomed to die, but at the very least he could now die with somewhat of a clear conscience. He begged the committee to keep him safe from any mob, for he knew that on many occasions, particularly in the South, a mob would mutilate and burn the body after the hanging. Ellis Craft was then sent for. He was found at his boardinghouse and taken into the presence of Ellis, who repeated the same story in his presence. Craft heard him through, and then said: "George, how can you tell such a lie?" But Ellis contended that it was true and that Craft knew it was true. Neal was then sent for and found at work in the rolling mill. He was also brought in, and Ellis reiterated the same in his presence. He, too, denied knowing anything about it.[63]

All three were white men, and each lived in Geiger's Addition near the vicinity of the Gibbons house. George Ellis was twenty-seven years old and had been married for a little over a year, having no children. He stood about five feet, nine inches tall, was stoutly built and had thinning hair and a mustache. He was described by his landlord as a good tenant and a very industrious young man who always seemed to conduct himself in a proper manner. William Neal, the largest of the three men at five feet, eleven inches tall, was twenty-five years old and married to Sarah Rice; together they had three small children.[64] Neal portrayed himself in a smiling, devil-may-care manner and apparently failed to appreciate his terrible position.[65]

Ellis Craft, who appeared to be the ringleader, was twenty-seven years old and never married. Craft stood five feet, six inches tall with a medium build, dark complexion, dark hair and a mustache. He seemed to have led a wild and reckless life. He had been previously arrested twice by Town Marshal J.C. Whitten and several times in Catlettsburg for disorderly conduct. Three times he had been convicted of criminal intercourse with young girls and had to leave the county for over a year. He shot at a businessman named Proctor about four months earlier when Proctor came to the defense of his wife after Craft had made lewd advances toward her. Yet he had always managed to escape all action against him. He was described as a rough, uncouth person whose conversation was known to have been vulgar among his companions.[66]

Craft and Ellis were at once taken to the Catlettsburg jail, and Neal was guarded until the next morning, when he was slipped out the back way and taken to Catlettsburg. All three were put in jail together, and Ellis, who (as he thought) was at the mercy of Craft, went back on his statement and said he did not know why he had made it. Poor, cowardly Ellis! He appeared to be completely under the control of Craft. This denial of his statement was in strict accordance with his confession, in which he said that Craft forced him go to the Gibbons house that night. The mistake of having the three suspects jailed together was soon realized, so Ellis was quickly conveyed by Boyd County sheriff John Kouns and a posse to the Greenup County jail for his own protection. While there, Ellis was observed pacing the floor and thought to have been feigning craziness, as he was heard to have uttered the most unearthly moans and groans.[67]

On the following morning after the arrests had been made, the greatest excitement prevailed on hearing the report that three men had been arrested and one of them had confessed. Businessmen shut up their stores; mechanics closed their shops. In fact, business of all kinds was, with one accord, dropped and, for the time, forgotten. The rolling mill and nail factory closed operations as suddenly as if there had been a blow-up. In a very short time after the news was spread, the streets were lined with people standing in squads, with the one theme of conversation. Everybody was quiet as a funeral, only low conversations to be heard in the crowds. Mob law was discussed from every standpoint, with the newspapers continually inciting the populace.[68]

> *People Flocking from All Points to the Jail Where the Prisoners Are Confined. Intense Excitement at Catlettsburg, where a Lynching Is Expected.*
> —Cincinnati Enquirer, *January 4, 1882*

> *Judge Lynch Will Preside They Are in the Catlettsburg Jail. Lynching Is Expected Tonight.*
> —Courier-Journal, *Louisville, KY, January 4, 1882*

Many citizens who probably never favored mobs before spoke favorably of it now, but all agreed that evidence must be positive before anything was done. The bodies of the three murdered children were exhumed by order of Marshall Heflin and the wounds were reexamined. The findings agreed with what was initially reported and the wounds corresponded exactly with the statements of George Ellis about their positions when the murderous blows were struck. The bodies were then reinterred in three separate graves.[69]

6

THE RIVER CHASE

Arrangements were made for the examining trial to be held five miles from Ashland at the county seat, Catlettsburg, at 1:00 p.m. that afternoon [Wednesday, January 4, 1882]. The people at once started out in buggies, hacks, wagons, on horseback, on the train and afoot, until it looked as if Ashland was to be cleared of its inhabitants. At noon, the Chattaroi Railway ran a special train to take up what people were left. About 250 persons went up on that train. Everybody was anxious to see the result of the examining trial. On their arrival at Catlettsburg, the excitement was about as great there as it was in Ashland. Business was suspended for the time, and a great portion of the citizens were gathered at the courthouse. The court was opened by County Judge Samuel S. Savage at 2:00 p.m. Before the opening of court, Circuit Judge George N. Brown had made a few remarks, saying he wanted everything done according to law so the opportunity might be afforded to bring out all the facts. He also noted that a special term of court was called for January 16, at which time justice would be meted out.[70]

The prisoners were then ordered into court. The crowded aisles were cleared. All eyes were turned to the door to get a sight of the prisoners, to see if they were really men or if they were demons in human form. After some consultation, it was thought best to defer the examining trial until the next day, in order to allow time to obtain witnesses. Disappointment reigned as the crowd dispersed and people returned to their homes and businesses to wait until the next day when they would once again return to the Catlettsburg courthouse. It was expected by some that the prisoners would be lynched during the night, but no attempt was made in that direction.[71]

The next morning, a rumor was carried to Catlettsburg that a mob was being organized at Ashland and would be up on the 1:00 p.m. train to hang the prisoners. As mob and lynching rumors were afloat, many citizens of Ashland were determined to repel any efforts at vigilante justice in favor of justice according to the law. The news of a possible organized mob reached the ears of Judge Brown, and after a brief consultation with County Judge Savage and the defense and prosecuting attorneys, he at once arranged to get the prisoners away. They were to be taken from Catlettsburg down the Ohio River to Maysville under the charge of Sheriff Kouns and his fifty-man posse. The steamer *Mountain Girl* was chartered for the occasion.[72]

Here, we give place to editor Huff and his account of the next episode in this intriguing drama.

The prisoners were slipped from the jail to the boat. And as the prisoners and their guards were waiting for sufficient steam to run the *Mountain Girl* down the Ohio, the whistle of the locomotive on the Chattaroi that once again carried the Ashland crowd to Catlettsburg was heard. "What will we do?" was asked by all. The train drew nearer, and as it reached the depot, the crowd rushed from the train and started for the courthouse. The sight of the crowd frightened the guards at the boat, who thought the Ashland people had come with vengeance, swift and sure. Something must be done! The Catlettsburg ferryboat was near at hand, with steam already up. The willing prisoners were hurried on board the ferryboat, as there was no time to wait for the *Mountain Girl* to get up enough steam, and orders were given to run for life. The people who came from Ashland to hear the trial saw the accused were on the boat leaving the wharf. She headed out to the current of the river and started down. This caused considerable commotion, and with one accord the people made a rush for the wharf. What's going on? What is happening? Where are they taking the prisoners? No one knew what to do. A great measure of chaos ensued. Cries could be heard from among the throng at the wharf directed toward the ferry, "Come back!" "Bring them back!" "Here is the place to keep them and try them!" The *Mountain Girl* yet had no steam up, but she was soon boarded by a few dozen members of the Ashland crowd and steam was soon raised. The officers of the steamer were assured there was no intention to harm the prisoners, but only to bring them back and keep them in the county jail until they could be fairly tried by law. So, off she went in hot pursuit of the ferryboat. By then, the ferryboat had nearly a two-mile head start down the river, but the much faster *Mountain Girl* was sure to catch up by the time the ferry had reached Ashland.

The next thing to be done was for everyone else to hurry to Ashland, as it was supposed that the *Mountain Girl* would overtake the ferryboat at this point, and a rush was made. The train was backed down. People who were on their way up to Catlettsburg turned their course around, all anxious to see the ferryboat overtaken and the prisoners brought back. And the excitement was increased by the expectation of some that they would be hanged as soon as caught. For the terrible crimes that had been committed were all that the people felt able to stand. And to add to this, the thought there might have been a plot to get the prisoners away where they might escape, was like pouring oil on the fire. Then the race itself was on such a chase that would excite everybody who could get excited.

As the chilling wind made their eyes squint and the cold droplets of Ohio River water gently sprayed their faces, the pursuers aboard the faster steamer finally got the ferryboat in their sights. And sure enough, just above Ashland, the *Mountain Girl* hailed the ferryboat and was answered. The people along the road and the riverbank could see their stacks and the smoke as they came together, where they lay about long enough to change prisoners and guards from one to the other. Then the *Mountain Girl* struck out for the Ashland wharf. The news quickly spread all over town that the boat was coming with the prisoners. A general rush was made for the bank to see them brought off the boat. But, lo and behold! The prisoners were not there. Unbeknownst to the men aboard the *Mountain Girl*, and the waiting crowd, the ferryboat had been met at some point up the river by another steamer, the *Mountain Boy*, and had transferred them and their guards, who were then on their downward way to Maysville. And then, as about two thousand people who had gathered at the grade and found they were tricked, cast their eyes downstream, only to see the smoke of the boat that had taken the prisoners, and too far ahead to be caught. And it was about at that same location the *Mountain Boy* was met with the steamer *Hudson*, which was on its way to Catlettsburg carrying twenty-five Maysville Guards who had been ordered by Kentucky Governor Luke P. Blackburn to protect the prisoners.

Here, words fail to give anything like a faint description of the disappointed people. They ran hither and thither. Plan after plan was hastily suggested, only to fail for the lack of some means of carrying them out. The river chase was abandoned and all hope to bring the prisoners back soon faded.[73]

One newspaper correspondent said he learned on good authority that a mob had been organized the previous night to hang the prisoners on this day, but it was not composed of Ashland people. Yet the deed would have been done at the expense of the good name of that city. It was widely known that roving bands of Regulators still operated in the region.[74]

Reports of roving bands of Regulators were documented by John E. Kleber in *The Kentucky Encyclopedia*, 1992:

> *The lawlessness that plagued Kentucky after the Civil War led to frequent outbreaks of vigilantism throughout the state. The majority of these organizations described themselves as "Regulators"—a term popularized by vigilantes on the southern frontier before the Revolutionary War. Although generally local and sporadic in nature, postwar vigilantism sparked a popular uprising that swept through northeastern Kentucky in 1879–1881.*
>
> *The uprising began in Elliott County, where outlaws in 1877 had burned a portion of Sandy Hook, the county seat. In September 1879, following a wave of crime marked by violence against women, the citizens of Elliott banded together and took it into their own hands to enforce the laws. In a proclamation to the people, "Judge Lynch" warned that lawlessness would no longer be tolerated. On the night of October 20, 1879, two hundred armed Regulators dragged two alleged outlaws from the Elliott County jail and hanged them on the courthouse grounds. The lynchings inaugurated a reign of terror against all suspected lawbreakers and undesirables in the region. Masked horseback riders whipped many victims and drove them out of the area. The vigilantes also punished many men and women accused of violating the moral standards of the community.*
>
> *By the spring of 1880, the movement had spread to the neighboring counties of Morgan, Rowan, Carter, Boyd, and Lawrence. On the night of March 17, 1880, the Elliott County organization claimed two more victims during a raid in Carter County. Openly defying the authorities, the Lawrence County Regulators forcibly rescued several jailed members in Louisa and Catlettsburg.*
>
> *Despite frequent death threats, Judge James E. Stewart of the 16th judicial district vowed to uphold the law against the Regulators and called on Gov. Luke P. Blackburn (1879–83) for state troops. Stewart's firm stand, the threat of military force, and the promise of executive clemency for Regulators who voluntarily surrendered broke the back of the movement. On May 28, 1880, over two hundred Lawrence and Carter County Regulators surrendered to Judge Stewart at Louisa. The voluntary disbanding of the Elliott and Morgan County organizations in July marked the end of the*

uprising, although outbreaks of terrorism in the region continued until 1881. Governor Blackburn subsequently pardoned hundreds of former Regulators throughout the region. Nevertheless, isolated acts of vigilantism continued to occur in the area until the early twentieth century.

Remarkable for the numbers involved, the Regulator uprising was defended by many as a necessary evil when the legal system failed to curb lawlessness. But the extreme violence that characterized the movement succeeded only in reinforcing the perception of late nineteenth century Kentucky as a lawless, violent society.[75] [emphasis added]

It is difficult to blame Judge Brown for taking the action of removing the prisoners. He could not have known whether the threats of mob violence were legitimate, but the people of Ashland felt they had been terribly wronged—not only because the prisoners had been taken away where they might have a better chance to escape but also on account of the way it would look to people abroad who would naturally suppose by the act of the river chase that mob law prevailed in Boyd County, and especially in Ashland. It seemed that the only way mob violence could be prevented was by a trick of the authorities to get the prisoners to another part of the state. Yet it had never been known of an instance where the people here have acted as coolly and deliberately, and at the same time as sensibly and determined, under such trying circumstances, as the people here have all through these exciting times. All that had been demanded was a speedy trial, and that without equivocation. This would have satisfied the people, and nothing short of it. It is a remarkable fact that through all the excitement, drinking men kept sober, there having been less drinking than ordinary, and all the crowds attending court were as orderly as though they were attending church. Even during the excitement of the race, when the people thought the prisoners were caught, an agreement was being signed not to do anything to the prisoners but return them to the jail. From all that could be learned, it was a pre-concerted arrangement to have them taken away, as they were met by twenty-five soldiers, who returned with them to Maysville.[76]

Disillusioned and somewhat embarrassed, the Ashland civic leaders called for a public meeting, and Mayor John Means addressed the citizens:

Citizens of Ashland! The trial of three prisoners accused of murder, rape and arson in our city has been set to begin on Wednesday next. By the perpetration of these crimes, and since the time, your patience and forbearance have been sorely tried, and to your honor have you not been found wanting. On Thursday last it was reported that a mob had started from our city to punish the men, without trial and without regard to law. This was false; so utterly without foundation that you justly felt indignant that it had been believed. Remember, that none know the people of Ashland as well as we know ourselves. Relying on your further patience and good judgment, a meeting will be held on Monday, January 9, at 2 o'clock p.m. in Geiger, Powell & Ferguson's Hall, to take such steps as will assure all people that we favor the enforcement of law and will lend our aid to the civil authorities, thereby repelling all statements to the contrary circulated to the prejudice of our good name.[77]

At that meeting on the following Monday, a resolutions committee was appointed, and the following resolutions were adopted by the citizens:

Whereas, a most atrocious and bloody crime has been perpetrated in our midst, which has aroused every citizen of this community to the importance of discovering, if possible, the guilty party or parties, and bringing them to justice; and

Whereas, the people have contributed of their means in order that the murderers might be captured and tried by the laws of our state, and if found guilty the punishment due their crime be meted out to them speedily, thereby ridding this community of the miscreants; and

Whereas, through the means set on foot by the citizens, three persons are under arrest, accused as the perpetrators of the crime; and

Whereas, the zeal of the people in assisting in bringing to justice the accused, and eagerness to have them speedily tried, and if found guilty, punished has been misconstrued and misrepresented by newspaper correspondents and others, who evidently do not understand the people of Boyd County and especially the citizens of Ashland and vicinity, who have taken such a deep interest in this matter; and

Whereas, the citizens of that part of the county, have been heralded abroad as a mob, and as being ready to lynch the accused without judge or jury or benefit of clergy; and

Whereas, the good name of this community has been sought to be tarnished, as indicated, and in order to refute the erroneous impressions which have gone out, branding us as a lawless people, and in order to show to our fellow citizens of the county and state and our neighbors of Ohio and West Va., that we are not only an order loving, and law abiding people, but that we are ready, if need be, to assist the civil authorities in every way, therefore be it

Resolved, 1st, That we approve the call for this meeting of the citizens of Ashland by our fellow citizens and acting Mayor John Means.

Resolved, 2nd, That we hereby express our belief that the civil authorities can have, if desired, the hearty cooperation of every citizen in this community to assist them in maintaining the peace and protecting the prisoners, without the interposition of the military.

Resolved, 3rd, That as a further assurance to civil authorities we hereby tender them our services for the protection of the prisoners, to the end that the accused may have a fair trial, the present excitement allayed, and good order maintained, and that Judge Brown be requested to ask the Governor to recall the military.

Resolved, 4th, That the meeting heartily commend the prudence and zeal with which the citizens committee of three have acted on ferreting out the perpetrators of this awful crime and we hereby express our opinion that in the selection of John Russell, John Calder and A.C. Campbell, no better or more efficient citizens could have been selected, as the result of their work so far has abundantly proved.

Resolved, 5th, That for their untiring and zealous efforts in ferreting out the perpetrators of the foul murder in our midst, James Heflin and J.C. Whitten have our sincere thanks.[78]

A list was then compiled of names of the men who pledged their assistance to protect the prisoners as necessary to grant them fair trials. The local press of Kentucky, Ohio and West Virginia were requested to publish the resolutions and proceedings of this meeting to show Ashland's commitment to law and order and its capability of handling its own affairs. A committee of four men (John Hager, S. Casebolt, R.D. Callihan and Al Mellor) was appointed to present a copy of these resolutions to Judge Brown at Catlettsburg.[79]

These men informed the judge there was no intention to mob the prisoners, and if he would have them returned, they would be protected at no expense to the state or county. But the committee soon returned and reported having been treated with contempt by Judge Brown. If only Judge Brown would have accepted their pledge, perhaps the following dreadful events in this drama might have been avoided. But he refused to accept their pledge, and when a second committee went up to plead with the judge, he accused them of being part of a mob and one as being the mob leader. Some sharp words followed, after which Judge Brown ultimately agreed to try to get a special act to have the court trial set a week sooner than the established date. This was satisfactory as far as speeding the matter along. But everyone knew the news would spread far and wide that the prisoners were run off to escape mobbing, and by this it would be understood Ashland was a community of outlaws and unable to manage its own affairs.[80]

Just as was feared and somewhat expected, the news spread far and near that the prisoners were removed to Maysville to get them away from the mob, which followed until turned back by the soldiers. And in the judge's request to grant a special term of court, Ashland was represented before the legislature as a mob. A special to the *Courier-Journal* said:

> *The House sent over to the Senate this morning the bill it had just passed for holding a special term of the court in Boyd County. Hon. Laban T. Moore rose and suggested that business then before the Senate be postponed for a few minutes to consider the House bill. He had, he said, just received a dispatch from Judge George N. Brown, of Boyd, calling earnestly for the special term. The perpetrators of this foulest crime that ever stained the history of Kentucky were now in jail and the howling mob surging around it, ready to break down not only the barriers of the law, but of the prison as well.*
>
> *By the general law the court could not be held under ten days, hence the necessity for this measure in order to preserve the State from another crime scarcely less horrible than the one which would soon be avenged. The bill passed both houses, and was a law in a few minutes, having received the Governor's signature. It provided that the Boyd County Circuit Court should meet Monday, January the 9th, and continue for twelve days.*[81]

And to make the thing complete, Major Allen was ordered to take charge of the Lexington Guards, McCreary Guards and Mason County Guards and go to Ashland. The order read as follows:

> *The command under Major John R. Allen will report to the Sheriff of Boyd county, and acting in conjunction with him, and subordinate to him in so far as to resist and prevent any unlawful rescue of the prisoners, will proceed with him by steamer to Ashland, in Boyd county. On arrival at Ashland the commanding officer will report to the Hon. George N. Brown, Judge of the Sixteenth Judicial District, and carry out his orders in maintaining and enforcing the civil power of the State. The commanding officer is directed*

> *to maintain the strictest military discipline and hold his men well in hand so as to present his full force against any body of men who may attempt to take the prisoners from the officers of the law.*[82]

The jail in Maysville was a rickety old building in an advanced stage of decay; escapes were almost a weekly occurrence. During their stay in the Maysville jail, the prisoners were seen by many curious visitors, and several different stories were started from what was said to be Ellis's confession. While there, Ellis was thought to have made some attempt at insanity, but he held to his initial confession and claimed Craft and Neal were both guilty.[83]

Usually in such cases the excitement abates, and the people, absorbed in business, seemingly forget and become indifferent. But not so in this instance. The more the people talked the more they became interested and determined to see the guilty punished. After the bill was passed that provided the Boyd County Circuit Court to convene on Monday, January 9, and Governor Blackburn had ordered Major John Allen to lead his troops to Ashland, he sent the following message to Ashland mayor John Means:

> *To Hon. John Means, the Acting Mayor of Ashland: I am gratified to be assured that the people of Boyd County will see to it that the persons charged with the murder of the Gibbons family shall have a fair and impartial trial. I am sorry to learn that there is a disposition upon the part of persons outside of the county to interfere with the due and proper consideration of the law. While I feel that I can safely rely on the people of Boyd, to whom great honor is due, I deem it best to send such a force as, with the aid of the people, will assure a fair trial, and if found guilty be punished by the law. This is due to the dignity of the law and the maintenance of civil authority, and as I am charged with the duty of seeing that the laws are faithfully executed, will see that it is done, and* will use the whole power of the State if need be. [emphasis added]
> *Luke P. Blackburn*[84]

The governor's message was artful and crafty at best, yet deceptive and two-faced at worst. He claimed to lay blame of the disruption of law and order on "persons outside of the county" but makes a bold threat to "use the whole power of the State if need be," to see that the laws are faithfully executed in Boyd County.

7
NEAL'S TRIAL

The special term of the Boyd County Circuit Court opened on Monday, January 9. A total of sixteen jurors were selected to serve on the grand jury, six of which were from Ashland proper. Those six were John Russell (foreman), J.L. Mead, D.D. Geiger, R. Adams, Hugh Means and L.E. Veyssie. The remaining persons were R. Prichard, R.B. Rigg, C.C. Eastham, R. Hatfield, William Lockwood, Martin Kazee, John Lockwood, J. McFinney, J.L. Mead, H. Blankenship and Joseph Mitchell. On January 11, the prisoners were again brought back to Catlettsburg, under the guard of soldiers. During this time, preparations were being made for the trial, which was to commence that week.[85]

On Thursday evening of that week, George Ellis was visited for a short time by his young wife. In the little time she had with him, she implored her husband to tell nothing but the truth:

> *"George,"* she said, *while hot tears blistered her cheeks and welled from her entreating eyes, "you can get forgiveness of God for your own sin, but if you tell a lie on William Neal and break the heart of his miserable wife and destroy the happiness of his three little children, your offense can never be atoned. I pray for you all the time and will continue to do so. I ran away with you to link my fate with yours, and this is the result. My heart is broken; but for God's sake save Mrs. Neal's, if her husband is innocent. I will never marry again. I will be true to your memory, but I want you to tell the truth as you hope for Heaven."*

> *Ellis was greatly affected by the burning words of his sobbing, heart-broken wife, and, brushing away the tears that dimmed his vision, said: "I will tell the truth, and am doing so when I say again that Neal and Craft are guilty of this thing."*[86]

The work of investigation went on for five days. Witnesses were brought forward for the prosecution and for the defense of each of the three men accused. Attorneys for Neal and Craft asked for, and were granted, separate trials. Ellis was unable to afford an attorney, so the court assigned Captain D.K. Weis from Ashland to represent him. Everything was thoroughly investigated, and on the evening of the fifth day, indictments were brought against William Neal and Ellis Craft for conspiracy and murder along with three indictments against George Ellis for murder. Large crowds had gathered in and around the courtroom each day, and good order had prevailed. William Neal was the first of the three to be tried, and his trial was set on Monday, January 16, for the murder of Emma Carico. The following are the names of the jury members who tried the case: John McDyer, John Allen, J.P. Ranking, Philip S. Fannin, L.C. Hazlett, Elza Rucker, Marion Hatten, C.P. Calwell, William Prichard, David Lockwood, Shepard Dixon and C. Prichard. The jury was pronounced a very good one.[87]

To represent him, William Neal chose the twenty-seven-year-old Catlettsburg attorney Thomas R. Brown, who was the son of Judge George N. Brown.[88] Assisting Thomas R. Brown in Neal's defense was his twenty-eight-year-old brother-in-law, attorney Alexander Lackey.[89] The prosecution consisted of thirty-three-year-old Commonwealth attorney Stephen G. Kinner[90] and the fifty-eight-year-old former Sixteenth District circuit judge William C. Ireland.[91] The courtroom was crowded with spectators eager to see the prisoners.[92] Judge Brown cautioned that if order was not maintained, he would clear the courtroom. The presence of the soldiers surrounding the courthouse was perceived by the citizens as intrusive and intimidating.

Craft and his attorneys bore a keen interest in Neal's trial, for they knew it would likely serve as a harbinger for Craft's trial, with many of the same witnesses voicing similar testimonies. The prosecution intended to prove beyond a reasonable doubt Neal's guilt on the strength of Ellis's confession and a mountain of corroborative circumstantial evidence. The indictments were read, and William Neal answered, "Not guilty." The trial lasted eight days, and the following is the substance of the testimony given in the case. Here again we give the sworn testimonies in this case as recorded by editor Huff, except where noted. The prosecution called its first witness.

After being sworn, George Ellis was asked how long he had lived in Ashland and when he had become acquainted with Ellis Craft and William Neal. He said he came to Ashland the previous May and went to work in the brickyard for Powell & House. And there he became acquainted with Craft and Neal. To the questions by the prosecution, Ellis gave direct, straightforward answers.

He was told to tell the jury what he knew about the murders of Emma Carico, Robert Gibbons and Fannie Gibbons, committed on the night of the December 23, which he did, in his own words, in substance what he had related in his confession at the time of his arrest.

> *I did not see Ellis Craft or William Neal during the day on December 23rd. I saw them late that night. They came to my house and called me. I was in bed and asked what they wanted. Craft told me to get up, that they wanted to see me. I did so and put on my clothes and boots and went out to the gate. Craft said, "You must go with us." I asked him where? He said, "to the Gibbons, and we will have some fun." I said it was too late, I would not go. They said I had to go, and Craft drew his revolver. Neal said, "bring him along." And we started. When we got inside at Gibbons' Craft picked up an ax and Neal got a crowbar from under the porch floor. Craft pried up the window and Neal was the first to go in. Craft went next. I did not want to go in, but Craft drew his revolver and said, "come on." And I did so. They took the ax and crowbar in the house with them. We passed through the front room to the second, or middle room where the girls and Robbie were asleep. Craft and Neal went to the bed where the girls were. Craft took hold of Fannie Gibbons and Neal of Emma Thomas. They stifled the girls by putting their hands over their mouths and choking them. The noise awakened Robbie who was sleeping on a lounge in the same room. Craft, who had choked Fannie Gibbons most to death, left her and struck Robbie in the head with an ax and killed him, and then returned to the bed. Neal dragged Emma Thomas off the bed on the floor and Craft ordered me to hold Miss Thomas until Neal accomplished his purpose, which I did. After Neal let her go, she began to raise up, crying, and said she was going home to tell her mother. Neal said, "I guess not," and struck her on the head with the crowbar and she fell back on the floor dead. Craft ordered me to come and help him. I went to the bed and put my hand on Miss Gibbons' shoulder, and Craft outraged her. After which he got up, got the ax, and killed her. Craft said to me, "you have done none of the killing, but you must have some hand in it." He ordered me to get the coal-oil can*

and pour it over the dead bodies of the girls. I did so, and Craft set them on fire, and we left the house. When we got out, we separated. I went home; I don't know where they went.[93]

The ax and crowbar were brought forward and examined by the witness. Ellis recognized the old ax as being the one used in the murder of two of the children, Robert Gibbons being struck by Craft with the poll of the ax and Fannie, he thought, with the side of the ax. He also knew the crowbar to be the same one used by Neal to murder Emma Carico. She was struck on the head with the small end, on which the hair of the girl was still to be seen.

The cross-examination somewhat frustrated the witness, although in substance it amounted to about the same he had before stated, the differences being in the conversations had with Neal. He said there had been no arrangement made between him and Craft and Neal, but Craft and Neal had both said what they intended to do with the girls. Craft said he intended to take Fannie Gibbons a Christmas gift on Christmas Eve night, and he had told Craft not to take it until Christmas morning.

Ellis continued:

The next Sunday (Christmas Day) morning I was near the burned house, when Craft came along and asked me to take a walk. We then walked out beyond the cemetery where we were met by Neal; after some talk on the subject of the murder, they told me I must sign a pledge that I would not tell. I said, "I will see about it." They said I could have until Saturday night to sign it, and if I did not sign it by that time they would stretch my neck. I afterward had another conversation with Neal on the subject, at the rolling-mill, in which Neal asked me if I had made up my mind to sign the pledge. I said I would see about it. Neal told me I had better do it. I was at the Gibbons house that night about an hour or hour and a half and could not sleep when I came back for thinking of the terrible crime I had committed.

The defense attorney asked Ellis if he was lying. He said he was not. The attorney then asked him, "Didn't you strike the boy yourself with the ax?"

He answered very promptly, "I did not."

"Didn't you kill one of the girls?" the attorney demanded.

"I did not."

The attorney continued to grill Ellis. "Have you told nothing but the truth in this case?"

"I have told the truth. As God as my judge!"

"Do you then believe in the existence of God?"

"I do, and I feel that I can appear before him free from the stain of the blow. I think I have told all I know. I first talked with Mr. John B. Powell about the affair. I told him I thought I could straighten the thing up. He asked me to go with him to the Aldine Hotel. There I met the Committee, to whom I told what I knew."

Ellis continued, "I am very sure it was Ellis Craft and William Neal that called at my house for me that night." He asserted,

> *I only laid my three fingers on the girls while Craft and Neal outraged them. Neal carried the crowbar and put it out at the front window. Craft left the ax in the house. I did not have the ax in my hand. Craft carried the ax in his left hand and pistol in his right. After the crime had been committed Craft told me to go and bring the oil and said I must have something to do in this. Craft followed me to the kitchen then stepped back, and I followed with the oil. Neal said something had to be done or it would get out.*

When asked how many doors he went through to get the oil, he said he was so frightened he did not know.

Ellis continued,

> *That day* [speaking of the day he had made his confession to the Citizens Committee] *I only told what I heard Neal and Craft say in the brickyard. At night I confessed, and think it was taken down by Mr. Campbell, who was writing while I was telling. The confession as read was about as I gave it to the best of my recollection. I was mistaken if I said the Thomas girl was struck with the big end of crowbar, for she was struck with the round end.*

Ellis was then asked about statements he had made in the presence of certain people while at the Maysville jail, when it was reported he had said both Craft and Neal were innocent. "I was talked to by a number of people while in that jail," Ellis said. "I do not remember all I said on various occasions. I was very much confused and excited most of the time."[94] By all accounts, Ellis had sustained himself very well during the cross-examination of the defense.

Drs. Martin, Wade and Tiernan all testified to about the same—they believed rape had been committed on both girls. They agreed the rupture of hymen could not have resulted from the burning of the bodies. Both bodies were badly burned about the lower parts, and from all appearance, coal oil had been used in the burning. They believed from the shape of the wounds that Robert Gibbons's head was crushed with the poll of an ax. Fannie Gibbons's head might have been mashed with an ax, but from the shape of the wound it could have been done with a crowbar. They gave all the particulars of the examination made by them the morning of the murder and also at the second examination. They showed the jury what part of the heads were crushed and the shape of the wounds.

Caroline Thomas, Emma Carico's mother, was next called. As she walked down the aisle toward the witness stand, a death-like silence prevailed. It required a great effort for this heartbroken mother to suppress her sorrow and tears, but she did it.[95]

She said she lived nearly opposite the Gibbons house and confirmed that her daughter, Emma, went to the Gibbons house about half-past six on the night of the murder by request of Martha Gibbons, who had gone to Ironton that evening.

> *I was up that morning about half-past four and looked toward the Gibbons' house but saw no fire. Fifteen minutes before six, I looked in that direction again and saw fire in the middle room through a side window. I then ran to the house and went around to the side door but could not get in. I came back to the front and went in through a window. I went to the bed in the front room but found there was no one in the bed. I stumbled over a pillow on the floor and went to the middle door but found it hard to open. I looked in and saw the room was full of smoke and so dark I could see nothing in the room but the lamp burning on the sewing machine. I then ran out and gave the alarm. The first one that came was Joe Arthur. Soon afterward several others were there, among whom were George Faulkner, J.W. House and John Mead. I stayed until the bodies were carried out, then went home.*

She said her daughter Emma was fourteen years old and large for her age, and she and Fannie Gibbons went to school together. Thomas said she had been acquainted with William Neal four years and Neal was well acquainted with her family. During her testimony, Mrs. Thomas, at times, could scarcely overcome her grief.

George Faulkner said he lived opposite the Gibbons house.

> *I am acquainted with the Gibbons family and knew them to be poor people. I heard the alarm of fire about 6 o'clock and heard two voices. I knew one to be that of Joe Arthur. I went over, taking a bucket of water with me. I broke*

> *in the window next to where the lounge sat and felt on the lounge for Robbie but found he was not there. I then went around to the other window next to the bed where the girls slept. I broke that window in with an ax; think it was a double-bitted ax. I could see one of the bodies with a hand up.*

He did not see William Neal at the fire.

John W. House said he was the third person at the fire and took the bodies out of the house. He located the bodies just where Ellis said they were left:

> *The bed sat next to the stairs, with its head toward the side of the house. I found the body of Emma Carico near the window and tried to lift the body out but could not do so. Afterward I went in the house and searched around in the dark and found the body of Fannie Gibbons on the bed covered up with burning bed clothes. I took her out at the lower side window. I then made a search for the other bodies. I found an oil can on the floor and found the body of Robbie Gibbons under the stairs; dragged it out on the side of the porch; and was afterwards assisted by Cyrus Wilson in carrying the body away. I do not remember how we got the body of Emma Carico out of the building. I did not see William Neal at the fire until after sunrise, when he was standing, with both hands in his pockets, about fifty yards from the burned house. I first saw a crowbar in a crack of the fence, with hair of Emma Carico on it. I did not see the ax until the next day; had blood and short hair on the poll. Robbie had his shirt on, and it was up around his neck; his drawers were only on one leg.*

Henry Culbertson worked at the muck shears at the Norton Iron Works. He testified:

> *I live in Ashland near the Norton Iron Works. I know William Neal, and he was working with me last December. There was no work going on the day after the tragedy. On the following Monday morning after the murder Neal was not on time at his work. I heard Neal say that he did not like to live in Geiger's addition for fear he would be arrested. I told him he ought not to talk that way.*

John Jacobs said he was well acquainted with William Neal and added:

> *I went to Neal's after him the Monday morning he was late for work but did not find him at home, but then found him at work when I went back*

and had some conversation with him on the subject of the murder, in which Neal said he never knew of anything he hated so badly as he did this. And that he hated to live in the town for fear some one would think it was him. I told him he should not talk so, if he was not guilty, he was in no danger. At that Neal said, "God knows I am not guilty."

Charles Venz knew William Neal. He said he lived forty or fifty yards from where Neal lived, in Geiger's Addition. He noted:

I was at the fire after the children had been taken out and the house about burned down. I went downtown with Neal and others that same morning. On the way I heard Neal say he bet the parties that committed the crime were in the crowd that morning at the fire. And at another time, in the mill, Neal asked me if I thought anyone would hurt him if he stayed there and worked. I said "No." On the day of the funeral of the murdered children, Neal's wife and children left home and I heard that they went to her father's. And I saw Neal's family as they left on that Monday morning. The children were poorly clad. I asked Neal to stay with me. Neal said he would go down in town with his friends. I promised to come by and wake him in the morning in time to go to work. I went to find Neal, but he was not there.[96]

Venz, of German heritage, said he could not understand English very well. The attorney then asked him how he could be so certain about what Neal had said—he said he could understand what Neal said. He was then asked by Thomas Brown what it was he couldn't understand. He replied, "Your big talk." (At this, smatterings of laughter emanated through the courtroom.)

John Gibbons, Robbie and Fannie's father, testified:

Robbie had lost his left leg. I slightly knew Neal. I heard Neal remark to some parties standing on the railroad—a black and a white man—as Emma Thomas went by, that "Miss Thomas is a good-looking girl, and I would like to have intercourse with her." This conversation took place about the time of the Ashland Fair, and as I was coming up the railroad, I ran upon the parties and overheard what Neal said.

Gibbons recognized the crowbar and kept it under the house near the porch. He did not know the ax.

Jacob Burk lived on Catlett's Creek and also testified:

> *I know William Neal. I live on Catlett's Creek, about a mile from Hiram Rice, Neal's father-in-law. I saw Neal on Christmas morning after the murder, at my house, on his way to his father-in-law's. Neal told me about the murder, and said he heard it was done with an ax and crowbar. I saw Neal again the next Monday week and talked about the reward offered for the arrest of the perpetrators.*

Alexander Chaffin lived with Jacob Burk and corroborated Burk's testimony:

> *I saw Neal there on Christmas morning, about 11 o'clock. I saw him there the Monday week and joked with him about arresting the perpetrators and getting the reward. Neal said if he was the one he wouldn't be afraid of a dozen like me. Neal said the tracks of three men were found where they had gone across the bottom and over the riverbank.*

Frank Compton lived on the road between Hiram Rice's and Ashland and was an uncle of Neal's wife:

> *I think I heard of the murder on the next Monday. Neal was at my house on the following Saturday night and said he was going to Hiram Rice's, but did not go. Through the night Neal would look around toward the door. He lay down on the bed with me and got up about 4 o'clock. John Keen offered to lend Neal his overcoat but said he did not need it.*

Jane Compton said William Neal stopped at her house on the Saturday night before New Year's, on his way to Hiram Rice's. She added:

> *He stayed till after supper and at bedtime I told him that I would ask him to stay all night but had no place for him to sleep. Neal said he hated to go so late. John Keen offered to lend him his overcoat, but Neal said that he did not want it, that he couldn't run good with it on. Neal was often at my house and never wanted to leave, and he stayed that night, talking and singing with the young folks like he always did—saw no difference in his actions. Neal laid down before the fire. I told him to go to bed. He then went to bed with Compton and got up the next morning at 4 o'clock and started away about daylight.*

William McMullan said he lived below the Gibbons house and that on the night before the fire, Robbie Gibbons came home as he always did. McMullan was at the fire at about 6:00 a.m. but did not see William Neal. The witness did see an ax with short hair—hair that resembled Robbie Gibbons's—on the poll. He said he attended the funeral the day after Christmas and saw Ellis Craft there.

J.B. Powell said he saw the fire about six o'clock that morning but did not go until about seven. He said Geiger, Powell and Ferguson owned the house where the Gibbonses had lived. He noted that he passed Neal's house, which was about five hundred feet from the Gibbons house, on the same street, that morning. Powell said he saw Neal's children and noticed the door was partially open. "I did not see William Neal at the fire, but saw him at the store about 11 o'clock, at which time Neal told me he worked at the mill until late and was very tired and went to bed as soon as he got home, and did not awaken until the next morning when the light from the burning house was shining in his face."

Mrs. Simmons lived near the gate of the Ashland cemetery and testified:

> *I heard of the fire and murder the same morning it occurred. On Christmas day, Mrs. Carroll was at my house. I saw three men on the road beyond her house on that morning, standing very close together. I could not tell who they were from my house, but as they passed, I recognized Ellis Craft and William Neal. I did not know the other, but that he had on a light hat and pants, and dark coat, and thought it was George Ellis by the way he was dressed. They went on toward Ashland until out of sight. I've known Craft and Neal for several years and was sure it was between 10 and 11 o'clock when I saw them.*

Mrs. William Carroll was at Mrs. Simmons's on Christmas morning and added:

> *I saw three men standing close together and stood so long that it attracted my attention. I could not tell who they were from the distance they were away. As they passed the house, I knew Ellis Craft, but neither of the others, but Mrs. Simmons knew two and described the other one that neither of us knew and that he was wearing a light hat and pants and dark coat. I thought it was near 11 o'clock in the morning as they passed the house toward Geiger's addition. They went together until out of sight.*

William Carroll noted, "I saw George Ellis at the burned house on Sunday about noon, and he had on light hat and pants and dark coat."

A suit of old clothes was then brought in, which Carroll believed to be George Ellis's. J.B. Powell was then called to the stand and said he knew them to be the clothes worn by George Ellis before his arrest.

Henry Culbertson was re-called. He said Neal was arrested at half past nine or ten o'clock on Monday evening after New Year's. On the night of the arrest Culbertson said he had some trouble with the shears and had trouble keeping Neal at work. He said he noticed Neal was acting strangely that night.

Jacob Emmons said he went with Marshal Heflin to the mill to arrest William Neal and found him at work. "I told him there was a gentleman outside who wanted to see him. Neal then went out saying, 'I know what you want.' He was then arrested and taken away." (Neal's comment, "I know what you want," was understood by some as a confession of guilt, but Neal did not make a confession at that time. Sworn testimonies of Neal's conversations in the days following the murders, however, showed he feared he would become a suspect and eventually arrested.)

Thomas Bird, second engineer at the rolling mill, said he was well acquainted with Neal since he had been working at the mill, which was about a month. On the night of and previous to Neal's arrest, he appeared to be restless and would not stick to his work. He said when the shears would get out of order Neal would go and sit around and wait until sent for.

Sterling Gibbons, son of John Gibbons, testified that he was eleven years old, going on twelve, and was at Ironton with his mother the night their house was burned. He knew the old ax, as he had found it in the woods. The last time he remembered seeing it, it was near the kitchen door. After this, the commonwealth rested, and the defense would take the floor the following morning at 9:00 a.m.

Neal's defense attorneys initially attempted to thwart Ellis's accusation against their client but then shifted their efforts to the Christmas Day meeting Ellis alleged to have had with Craft and Neal near the cemetery. By their concern with the time and whereabouts of Craft on that day, they tried to disprove Ellis's account of the cemetery meeting, thereby creating a reasonable doubt regarding his whole testimony.

Mrs. George (Fanny) Ellis was the first witness called to the stand for the defense.

> *I live in Geiger's addition, and that on the night before Christmas Eve I was at home and went to bed about 7 o'clock. My husband, George Ellis, ate his*

supper at home, went to bed early, and was not out during the night that I knew of. I was awake at 12 and at 3 o'clock, and George was at home both times. I got up as the whistle blew and got breakfast ready. I did not know when George started to work, for he heard the alarm of fire and went there. I did not hear any hallooing about the house through the night. I was at home on Christmas morning, at breakfast about 7 o'clock. After breakfast George went up to the burned house, but not very long after he left the house, I saw him and Ellis Craft up at the burned house together. I did not get any dinner that day. George went downtown that afternoon. He would have had time to go to the cemetery and back during the time he was gone in the morning. There were a good many persons about the Thomas house.

At cross-examination, Mrs. Ellis said it was an hour from the time she saw George at the burned house until he returned, but it might have been longer. The question was asked if she had been thinking about how much time elapsed from the time George left until his return, and she said she had not.

Oliver Hampton testified, "I heard the conversation between George Ellis and A.C. Campbell in the hall at the jail on January 3. Ellis Craft was in the jail with him at the time. I heard George say that Craft and Neal were innocent of the crime and did not know what made him say they were guilty. George had said that something must have gone wrong with his mind."

The defense team member Alexander Lackey here produced in evidence several depositions of persons who were confined in the Mason County (Maysville) Jail when Craft, Neal and Ellis were there. These depositions asserted George Ellis had said in their presence that he, Neal and Craft had made prior plans to visit the Gibbonses the night of the murders.[97]

J.B. Powell said he was one of the owners of the Gibbons house and gave a long and full description of the house and their positions to each other in Geiger's Addition. He also examined a diagram of the house and thought it was about correct. He said Ellis came into the store on the same day Gibbons came back to town and claimed that he had said to Ellis: "Now, George, Gibbons has come back, and his skirts are clear, who will this thing fall on?" Powell then noticed Ellis's hand shake as he gave him some cigars. He said he then asked Ellis who he thought the guilty one was, and Ellis said he hardly knew but believed he could find out. He said Ellis was afraid of state's evidence, that there was no one but himself and his wife and the other two would be against him. Powell continued, "I then went out to hunt Marshal Heflin, who was in town hunting the thing up." He further said there was a great deal of excitement and money was raised to pay the expenses in arresting the parties who committed the crime. He said one Black man, Willis Hockerty, was arrested but soon afterward released. He said he had known Neal from a little boy and never heard anything bad about him.

Millard Bell testified, "I heard Ellis tell part of his confession. I heard him say to Craft, that he was telling the truth."

Edgar Hubbard said he passed the Gibbons house about fifteen minutes after three o'clock in the morning on his way to the mill and returned in about five minutes. He said he saw no fire or light about the house and that he had passed in twenty-five yards of the house.

Joseph Arthur said he was at the fire about six o'clock that morning and saw no one when he got there but Caroline Thomas. The crowbar was then shown to him, and he recognized it as being the one he picked up near the burning house and put over the fence the morning of the fire.

Lincoln House said he had been living in Portsmouth, Ohio, for about a year.

> *I came to my father's (J.W. House) in Geiger's addition, on Christmas Eve about 1 o'clock at night. Ellis Craft was at the house and ate breakfast at about 8 o'clock. After breakfast Craft killed a turkey, went out, and said he was going to town to get some cigars. I did not see him for an hour; he then showed me some cigars, candy and a cravat that he had bought. Craft was at the burned house about 6 o'clock and assisted in pushing down the chimney.*

On cross-examination, House was asked if he did not state before the grand jury that Craft was gone three or four hours in the morning. He said he did but had thought it over since and was now sure as to the length of time. He said he changed his mind about the length of what time had expired when he recalled Craft showing him the cigars and candy he had bought.

Oliver House, another son of J.W. House, said,

> *I live in Geiger's Addition with my father. I was at home the night before Christmas. Ellis Craft ate breakfast at our house that morning. After breakfast, Craft and I killed a turkey. Craft started out about 9 o'clock on Christmas morning and said he was going to town to get some cigars and would soon be back. I next saw him at the burned house. He asked me and my brother to go and help him feed, water and curry the horses. We did so and came back to the burned house and assisted in pushing down the chimney. I thought it was after or about 12 o'clock. I did not see Craft have any cigars.*

Richard House was employed in Shaw's store and there early Christmas morning until half-past noon. Ellis Craft was in the store that morning and bought cigars and candy, but House could not recollect what time of day he was there. He attested he kept the store open on Sunday morning but not all day.

Mary Vaughn said she lived in Geiger's Addition and was at home on Christmas morning. She said that she had been acquainted with George Ellis since he had been working for House. She further stated that she saw Ellis Craft pass through the Houses' garden about eleven o'clock and he gave her some candy for a Christmas gift.

Mrs. Horton said she lived on the road from Geiger's Addition to Ashland and she knew Craft. "He was at my house on Christmas morning to pay my husband for a trunk and to pay me for washing. It was before I had my dinner but could not tell what time it was. I never did any more washing for Craft after that. Craft had told me he had a pair of pants he wanted washed, but he never brought them."

Frank Butler said he lived halfway from Catlettsburg to Ashland. He added that he sat up at the wake at J.W. House's (where Robert and Fannie Gibbons's bodies were kept) on Christmas Eve and ate breakfast there on Christmas morning about eight o'clock. There he saw Craft at the breakfast table. When Butler had lain down about daylight, he thought Craft was on the same bed but was not sure.

Joseph Bartram said he lived in the Flatwoods and went from home to Ashland on Christmas morning, accompanied by John Hensley and Isaiah McAllister.

> *We met William Neal near the Ashland Cemetery about 9 o'clock and had a conversation with him. We were in sight of the Simmons' house which we passed by on our way to Ashland. Neal went toward the Flatwoods. At the time we were talking a woman appeared in the yard at the Simmons house, with a bucket of something in her hand, but did not know what it was. I saw no one at the Simmons house as we passed, the door was shut.*

On cross-examination, Bartram said he had breakfast about daylight and had come about one and a half miles when they were met by Neal. The trio asked, "Christmas gift! Have you got anything to drink?" Neal said no, that he had worked late and did not have time to go after any before he started. They then asked Neal if it was really so about the house and three children being burned in Ashland. Neal said it was true. Bartram, Hensley and McAllister were two or three hundred yards from the Simmons house at the time of the conversation, the bridge being between where they stood and the Simmons house.

John Hensley said he made his home on Keyser's Creek and he came from home to Ashland on Christmas morning in company with Joseph Bartram and Isaiah McAllister. He confirmed they had a conversation with Neal near the cemetery, between eight and nine o'clock that morning but could not say how long they talked. He did not see any one while there but saw a woman at the Simmons house as they passed. He said they went on to Ashland and Neal went toward Keyser's Creek.

Isaiah McAllister was not well acquainted with Neal, only knew him when he saw him. He went to Ashland in company with Joseph Bartram and John Hensley, and they met Neal between the hours of eight and nine o'clock, near the cemetery. McAllister said he saw a woman at Simmons house, and she had something in her hand. Then they parted, the three going toward Ashland and Neal going in the direction of Keyser's Creek; Neal had crossed the bridge when they met him.

J.W. House was re-called and said Craft was at his house Christmas Day. They ate breakfast at eight o'clock, and half an hour later Craft killed the turkey. He said Craft went to the burned house after breakfast and was absent until about ten o'clock, then went to Ashland. House said he thought Neal was a peaceable man.

Oliver Hampton, John Starkey and Samuel Copley testified to Neal's good reputation. The court adjourned at half past four until nine o'clock the following morning, at which time the defense would continue calling witnesses in defense of Neal.

Mrs. J.W. House testified,

> *Ellis Craft had boarded at my house since August up to the time of his arrest. On the night the corpses of the murdered children were at my house Craft sat up at the wake. He ate breakfast about 8 o'clock at my house the next morning, which was Christmas morning, and about 9 o'clock killed a turkey for me. After that he dressed and went away, said he was going after cigars. Ollie said, "You are going to Church," referring to a girl by the name of Lizzie Church. I think he was back again about 10 o'clock. I did not see the cravat or cigars but heard them talking about them in the room. I am positive Craft was at my house when Ball, Webb, and another gentleman were there to see the corpses.*

On cross-examination Mrs. House said, "There had been talk in the family about the time of the occurrences but had no agreement in fixing the time. We ate dinner a little after 12 o'clock, might have been half after or one o'clock, but I do not think it was so late as 1 p.m." She was asked to relate some circumstances by which she kept the time. She added:

> We ate breakfast at 8, Craft killed the turkey at 9, and went away a little later; came back about 10. He was in the house half or three-quarters of an hour, then went over to the burned house and came back to dinner. I think the turkey would cook in an hour and a half. I know I would have put the turkey on in time to get it done by dinner time. I was fixing dinner when the three men came. I do not think Mr. Bartram to be a very old man nor very young. On the morning of the fire I was aroused by someone hallooing and looked out and saw the light. I then went to the other side of the house and saw it was the Gibbons' house on fire. I first told Mr. House, then the children, and then went upstairs to awake my son and Craft in their room and told them Gibbons' house was on fire. They got up and Oliver came down first; Craft was looking for some of his clothing. Craft came down and said maybe it was the light from the furnace. I was over to the fire twice, and when I came back home the second time I went and examined Craft's clothes.

Henry Culbertson said, "William Neal worked with me on the night of the murder. We got done five minutes before 12 at night; then washed and chatted five or ten minutes and started home together. Neal had his lamp and dinner bucket in hand."

Martha Hood testified to Neal's whereabouts the night of the murders:

> I am William Neal's cousin by marriage. I had been living at William Neal's about three weeks and was there on the night of the murder. John Keen was there until fifteen minutes of 11 by Keen's watch (which was half an hour faster than mill time). Neal came home about an hour and a half afterward and went to bed. I had the toothache and did not go to sleep until after 12. I heard Neal snoring in the night and did not see anything uncommon in his manners. Neal did not go out anymore that night that I knew of. My tooth got easier and I went to sleep after twelve and slept soundly until daylight, when I was aroused by Mrs. Neal's hallooing "fire." Neal then got up, put on his boots and went to the fire; the building was falling in then.

On cross-examination, she said,

> I went to sleep after Neal came home and did not wake any more until the alarm of fire was given. He did not wake me up the morning of the fire. The Saturday Neal stayed at my mother's his wife was at her father's. I left Ashland because I was afraid to stay after the murder. Neal's wife went to her father's house because she was afraid to stay at home after the murder. Charley Venz generally came and waked Neal up to go to work. Venz called Neal the Monday morning after the fire, and they went off together. I am sure Neal was at home that Monday morning, and I am sure he and Venz went off together. Venz came in the house and waited until Neal got ready. Mr. Jacobs nor nobody else came to the house that morning.[98]

When Hood was re-examined by the defense, she said, "The night before Christmas I stayed at William Neal's and remained there until in the afternoon. We ate breakfast at Neal's about eight o'clock. Neal left about nine o'clock, and said he was going to Hiram Rice's."[99]

John Keen testified next:

> I live in Ashland. I was at William Neal's house the night before Christmas. I saw Martha Hood and Mrs. Neal. I left the house fifteen minutes after eleven o'clock by my watch, which was fifteen minutes faster than Ashland time. William Neal stayed at my father's the Monday night after Christmas. He slept with me that night. He said his wife had gone to her father's. The Saturday night before New Year's Neal and I went out to Frank Compton's and stayed all night. I was at William Neal's on Christmas night. I stayed all night. Neal got up on Monday morning about four o'clock; his time to go to work was about four o'clock.[100]

Elizabeth Keen was also questioned:

> I live in Ashland. I am William Neal's aunt. He came to my house to board on Monday night after the murder, to the best of my recollection. I can't recollect very well. I woke Bill on Tuesday morning. He was awful hard to wake. I woke him several times and told him to go to work. He slept on, and the girls went and shook him before he would get up.

On being asked if the murder had been talked about in the family, she said, "Yes, we all talked about it. Bill didn't talk any more than the rest, but everybody was talking about it." She was asked if she did not say before the grand jury that she did not allow it talked about in the family. She averred, "Yes, I did not allow them to, and would stop them when they began. It hurt me so bad I couldn't stand to hear about it." Keen was asked if Neal didn't tell her he was afraid that he would be suspicioned because his family was gone, and she confirmed: "Yes, and someone said there was no danger of that."

Hiram Rice testified: "Neal is my son-in-law. He came to my house on Christmas day, just as we were done dinner. I don't think it was as late as 12 o'clock when we had dinner. Neal stayed till sundown, was back again on the next Sunday morning and stayed until Monday morning."

Pierce Bartram added, "I live in Sandy City. On Christmas morning I went to J.W. House's and I saw Jack Webb, Bill Ball, Ellis Craft and some other young fellow there. This was about 11 o'clock. It was maybe fifteen minutes before or after 10 or 11, I do not know which. I went down the road to Ashland and then back in the evening. I was not alone any other time that morning."

Jack Webb spoke to the timing: "I was at Ashland on Christmas day; went to House's to see the murdered children. I think it was between 10 and 11 o'clock. For while there I heard someone say fifteen minutes after 10 or fifteen minutes before 11, I don't remember which. I saw Craft there sitting in a chair."

On cross-examination, Webb said: "I was first asked about the time I was there by Mr. Craft who sent me word that he wanted to see me, and then asked me what time it was when I was there. Old man Bartram was along as we came back from Ashland. I am sure it was not after 12 o'clock. I knew it by the clock and by the time since I left home."

Joseph Bartram added, "From Sandy City to Geiger's addition is three and one-half miles. When I met Neal over at the cemetery, he told me he was going to his father-in-law's, over on the creek."

The defense asked leave to introduce Craft—who was jointly indicted with Neal—as a witness. The prosecution objected, and the court sustained the objection. Here the defense for Neal closed its case.[101]

The prosecution took the floor with rebutting testimony and called Dr. S.W. Patton of Catlettsburg, who said:

> *I went to Ashland on horseback on Christmas day with Dave Chadwick to attend the postmortem examination of the murdered children. I started from home about 11 o'clock or a little after and as I went down, I overtook*

Pierce Bartram, Jack Webb and another man on the road by Dave Geiger's. I think it was then about 12 o'clock, or within a few minutes of it.

U.S. Deputy Marshal James Heflin and C.M. Williams of Maysville, plus a number of Mason County Guards took the stand to prove the characters of the witnesses (prisoners in the Maysville jail at the time Ellis, Neal and Craft were there) whose depositions were previously taken and read for the defense, all of whom swore these men were not entitled to belief on oath.[102]

Dave Chadwick testified, "I went to Ashland on Christmas day with Dr. Patton, and as we went, we passed Jack Webb, Pierce Bartram and another man on the road by Geiger's, about one mile from House's. We started from home after 11 o'clock and passed the men about 12."

At 3:30 p.m., attorney for the prosecution W.C. Ireland announced they were through, and the defense responded they had nothing further. The defense had examined thirty witnesses. The prisoner, Neal, was remanded to the guard, and the court adjourned until the next morning.

On Monday morning, January 23, 1882, the argument in the case of Neal began and was heard by the largest audience that had been present since the trial began. The large courtroom, main and side aisles and inside the bar were crowded with men eager to hear the instructions given by the court and the conclusions presented by the counsel to the jury. At 11:00 a.m., Thomas R. Brown took the floor for the defense and made a well-timed and ingenious speech, closing his argument at 2:45 p.m. It was indeed a fine effort, considering the disadvantage of having no real defense to rely on. He was followed by former judge W.C. Ireland in one of his greatest speeches; he destroyed every shadow of defense made.[103]

In the evening, Lackey delivered an able speech for the defense. The concluding speech, however, made by S.G. Kinner, commonwealth's attorney, claimed the closest attention of the jury court and audience for two hours. The speech was one of which Kinner may justly be proud, as it was spoken of in terms of the highest praise by all who heard it.[104]

The following are the instructions given to the jury by the court:

1. The Court instructs the jury if they believe from all the evidence, to the exclusion of all reasonable doubt, the accused William Neal, in Boyd County, and before the finding of the indictment, did willfully, feloniously and of his malice aforethought kill and murder Emma Carico by striking her on the head with an iron crowbar, a deadly weapon, and which blow was made by the said William Neal with the intent to kill the said Emma

Carico, and of which blow she then and there died, they will find him, the said William Neal, guilty of murder, as charged in the indictment, and fix his punishment with death, or confinement in the penitentiary for life, in the discretion of the Jury.

2. The jury are sole judges of the credibility of the witnesses, and of the consideration to be given to the testimony of each; and in determining the case or material questions in the case, the jury may consider all the facts and circumstances which the Court has permitted to be given and remain as evidence.

3. The law presumes the accused innocent, and it is the duty of the jury, if they can reasonably do so, to reconcile all the facts and circumstances of the case with that presumption; and the jury are not to find their verdict on a preponderance of the weight of testimony; but if the jury, upon all the evidence entertain a reasonable doubt of the guilt of the accused, or of any material fact necessary to establish his guilt then they should find the accused not guilty.

4. The burden of proof is upon the Commonwealth to establish by evidence to the exclusion of a reasonable doubt, the guilt of the accused, or any material fact in the case necessary to constitute his guilt.

5. The jury, in rendering their verdict, must be governed by the law given in the instructions of the Court, and the evidence permitted to go to them and not excluded, and to consider nothing outside of the same.[105]

On Tuesday morning, the eighth day of the trial, the jury members were sent to their room. After being out eighteen minutes, as Neal stood calmly facing the jury, the foreman, John McDyer, brought forth the following verdict: "We, the Jury, find the defendant, William Neal, guilty of willful murder, as charged in the indictment and fix his punishment with death." Neal then had a brief whispered conversation with his attorney, and as the guard ushered him out of the courtroom, he began to weep bitterly while proclaiming his innocence.[106]

Midway through Neal's trial, an unfortunate and terrifying incident occurred just across the river from Ashland in Ironton, Ohio. Two accused murderers, John Wagoner and William Zeek, were forcibly removed from the Ironton jail by a band of masked men. With a noose around his neck, the frightened Zeek offered a complete confession and was then delivered back to the safety of the jail. Wagoner, on the other hand, remained cool and collected, and having made no appeal for mercy he had his neck stretched until dead. The murderous mob was said to have been about fifty strong and well organized with military-style discipline. They spoke very little in low, disguised voices and referred to one another with numbered identities—"one, two, three, etc."[107]

The coroner's inquest over Wagoner's remains yielded nothing about the identities of any masked members of the lynching party, and any further investigation was deemed unlikely.[108] The news of the Ironton lynching increased the anxiety of the Boyd County citizens, the three Ashland prisoners, Major Allen and his military guards and Judge George N. Brown.

8

CRAFT'S TRIAL

The trial of Ellis Craft followed immediately after Neal's. Once again, the courtroom was filled to overflowing by concerned and curious spectators. Unlike Neal, Craft was able to garner a measure of financial support from relatives, which afforded him the benefit of representation by a more experienced attorney. Craft's older brother, Tilman Craft was a merchant in the grocery business and provided certain means in an effort to prove his brother's innocence.[109]

Roland C. Burns, the thirty-five-year-old son of former state senator John M. Burns, represented Craft. Citing legal technicalities, Burns made several attempts for a dismissal of the indictment against Craft. For one, Burns claimed one of the men who sat on the grand jury that returned the indictment, Martin Kazee, was not a resident housekeeper of Boyd County at the time he was summoned. Kazee was then sent for, brought into court and proved he was, at the time of finding the indictment, a bona fide housekeeper of Boyd County. After consideration, the court overruled the motion for dismissal and continued.[110]

Burns then set forth grounds for a change of venue, claiming Craft could not have a fair and impartial trial in Boyd County. The defense brought forth three witnesses who testified on behalf of the affidavit for a change of venue, one of whom was Hiram Rice, William Neal's father-in-law. The prosecution also brought forth three witnesses, one of whom was Pat Suddith, who testified he was aboard the *Mountain Girl* during the river chase and had heard no threats made to lynch the prisoners, only to bring them back and have them tried in Boyd County.[111]

After hearing all testimony for a change of venue, Judge Brown overruled the defendant's motion, and the selection of competent jurors began. Forty-four men were examined; five were excused by the prosecution, nineteen by the defense and eight by the court. The jury was completed at 5:30 p.m., and court adjourned until the next morning. The following named persons composed the jury in Craft's case: James McLaughlin, Thomas Brown, William Isaacs, J.W. Farmer, Benjamin Sweet, George Ross, Green Queen, W.L. Fannin, William Williams, James Twynam, John Higgins and C.C. Fowler. The indictment was read, charging Craft with the murder of Fannie Gibbons, to which he answered, "Not guilty."[112]

Many of the same witnesses were used, and the same testimony given as in Neal's trial, with a few exceptions. Since the trial of Neal, a bloody towel (sweat rag) allegedly belonging to him had been found hidden under a fence near the scene of the crime and close to a stream of water, where it was supposed the murderers washed their bloodstained hands after their brutal work.[113]

The following witness testimonies in this case were also recorded by editor Huff, except where noted.

Marshal Heflin produced the towel and said he had obtained it from Taylor Davis. He had then taken the towel to Henry Culbertson, with whom Neal was working the night of the murder, who gave a full description of the towel before he saw it.[114]

Culbertson said it was the same towel used by Neal the night the murder was committed, before he left the rolling mill. He said he remembered the towel so well because he had used the same towel on that night and held it up to the furnace to dry and noticed the blue stripe and the holes in the corner.[115]

John Black said he first saw the towel under the fence as he was walking on the bank holding to the fence to keep out of the mud, and he afterward came back with Taylor Davis, who took the towel from under the corner of the fence. The towel was found near Geigersville.[116]

Dr. W.S. Barnett was called as an expert and testified he had made the best examination of the bloody towel he could and was positive the stains on it were blood. The doctor was not able to say it was human blood by reason of decomposition.

Robert Hanner testified he worked in the brickyard with Craft and had heard him make remarks about Fannie Gibbons. Oliver House added that he had heard Craft say frequently he would like to carnally know Fannie

Gibbons, and he was going to make indecent proposals to her. He testified Craft was out late the night of the murder.[117]

Mrs. Simmons testified—in substance the same thing she had said at Neal's trial about seeing the three prisoners together near the cemetery on Christmas Day—but it bears repeating here:

> *I live just beyond the Ashland cemetery. I was at home in the forenoon of Christmas day. My sister-in-law was there. That morning I saw three men standing in the road very close together. They remained there for some time, so long that my attention was attracted, and I watched them. When they left where they were standing, they started in the direction of Ashland and passed by my house. I watched to see who they were, and I recognized one as Ellis Craft, another as William Neal, and the other, I thought, was George Ellis. I am well acquainted with Craft and Neal, both having boarded at my house. I think the third man was George Ellis.*[118]

The evidence for this defense team was mainly directed toward accounting for the whereabouts of Craft on the night of the murder and again to show it was impossible for him to have taken the walk on Christmas Day with Ellis, as alleged, to the point near the cemetery where the latter stated they met Neal and held the famous consultation.

Joseph Bartram, John Hensley and Isaiah McAllister testified to meeting Neal near the cemetery, where the alleged meeting was held between the murderers Sunday morning after the tragedy. On cross-examination, their evidence was considerably shaken.[119]

William Riggles said Ellis Craft was at his house with Maria Wallace on the Friday night before Christmas until between ten and eleven o'clock. Mrs. Burdett said Wallace lived at her house but went away with Ellis Craft on Friday night before Christmas and never returned.

Sarah Neal, the wife of William Neal, was called for defense. She testified that the bloodstained towel shown to her was not her husband's towel, and she had never seen it before.[120]

Ballard Faulkner, James Davis and Joshua Whittaker, who were confined in the Boyd County jail at the time Craft, Neal and Ellis were there, were put upon the stand and swore Ellis had declared that Craft was innocent of any participation in the murders.[121]

During the trial, one of the jurors received a letter, the contents of which are as follows:

The Ashland Tragedy

Ashland, Ky., January 31, 1882

Mr. B.F. Sweet—My Dear Sir: This case against these boys is all a fraud. Be careful with your decision. The people here are seeing into it and changing their opinion fast. A gentleman told me yesterday that he had good authority for saying that those women that swore to the meeting at the cemetery were bought by the detective. He is after the reward and nothing else. Public opinion in this town is fast changing in favor of the prisoners. God knows a man who is innocent ought not to suffer for this act. Keep this to yourself. You and I are good friends. The reason I write I feel I am doing right. What I know it is a put-up job. The first time I see you in town I will have a talk about it with you.
Merchant[122]

On Saturday afternoon, February 4, about three o'clock, the tenth day of the trial, the jury, after being out twenty minutes, brought in a verdict of guilty and fixed the penalty at death. After the verdict was pronounced, Craft made a short speech in which he declared his innocence. On the following Monday, February 6, at 10:30 a.m., the judge had Neal brought into court and pronounced the terrible sentence that he should be hanged until he was dead.

Before pronouncing the sentence, the judge asked: "Have you anything to say why sentence should not be passed?"

Neal replied, "Do you want me to tell it all?"

Judge Brown retorted, "I will not dictate what you are to say."

Neal then went on to say that on the night the murder was committed he was at work at the mill until near midnight and that he talked for a little while, then took his bucket and started home to his wife and children. He then ate a lunch and went to bed and knew nothing about it until next morning. The time of his execution was set for Friday, April 14, 1882, between sunrise and sunset.

On the following day, Ellis Craft was also sentenced and his execution also set for April 14. Before the sentence was pronounced, Craft was given permission to speak. The following is his speech:

The truth has not come out yet. If the truth had come out, I would not have to speak here today. It appears that someone has to hang, and it has as well be me as anyone else. The minds of the people have already been made up and someone must hang. Nothing could be too bad for the one who did it, but only to think of an innocent man being hung. Look at me; I want you all to look at me and see an honest man. I am glad to see so many here and I want you to remember my words, that I am innocent of the blood of those little children. Look at it for yourself; put yourself in my condition and then look at it. I wish some innocent person could take my place for a while and see how I feel. My mother and father raised me right. I have done the best I could. I have worked for my living. I can laugh to myself to think I am innocent, but it is hard to think an innocent man must hang. I am innocent of the blood of those little children. What good would it do me to deny it now? It would only be heaping sin upon sin, and there is no forgiveness after death. I am ready to die. I expect to go from this world to a better one. I will not have to pray for forgiveness for murdering those little children, for I never did it. If they were the last words I ever expected to utter—if I was on the gallows—I would say I am an innocent man.[123]

This finished up the cases of Neal and Craft, and the trial of George Ellis was set for the regular May term of court.

9

BURNETT'S THEORY

Without a dissenting voice, the verdicts were approved. This horrible crime was to be avenged by the law, and those who had offered opinions and were loud in their condemnation of the manner in which the courts had taken hold of the case now mentally apologized and vowed subjection in the future. With those two trials over, everyone looked forward to the next one. The people were satisfied. No trial was ever held in Northeastern Kentucky that attracted so much attention at home and abroad as those of William Neal and Ellis Craft.[124]

As expected, the soldier guards departed for their homes, and with them went Neal, Craft and Ellis. They were taken to Lexington and placed in jail. The excitement of the trials was succeeded by the calm of content, and judge, juries, attorneys and witnesses received their just due of praise. All had been faithful in their endeavor to hunt down this crime—not to prosecute innocent men, but to punish the guilty.[125]

The day of execution had been fixed for two, who were looked upon as being most guilty, and a feeling of leniency toward the third party pervaded the community. Nearly all joined in the opinion that some consideration was due to the one through whose evidence the others had been brought to justice. The evidence of Ellis in court had been satisfactory. The all-powerful points in his confession had been adhered to through the cross-examination and difficulties of the trials with such faithfulness that a kindly sentiment was felt for him by many who believed it would be wrong to hold a man responsible for physical cowardice. Few things had been developed to prove

Ellis had not been compelled to take part in the awful transaction by his strong-minded companions.[126]

Upon the three prisoners' arrival in Lexington, a great crowd of people had assembled to welcome the military guards home and to get a glimpse of the wrongdoers.[127] George Ellis was cuffed, shackled, kept in a dark cell and separated from the other two. Meanwhile, Neal and Craft were granted the privilege of the jail yard, where they were able to greet the visitors hospitably as they proclaimed their innocence at every opportunity in the matter. In Lexington, those two quickly became viewed as victims by a bleeding-heart public, and even heroes, while receiving up to three hundred visitors per day who would eagerly listen to their versions of the story and their pleas of innocence.[128]

The three had been in jail but a short time when those interested were startled by the finding of a coat smeared with blood—it was proven to be the property of Neal. The garment was found by some little boys under a bridge a short distance from the scene of the crime, and this, another mute witness, was allowed a place in the chain of evidence against the fiendish owner. Can the murderer hope for escape? Can the midnight-loving scoundrel avoid his doom when his own hands aid in his detection? When he rushed from the house, where his brain had chronicled every cry, every groan, every plea for mercy, every awful, gurgling, gasping death cry; his eyes had mirrored scenes of horror that could not but confuse, his intellect was distracted and he had lost his cunning. The hiding place for his coat was not secure.[129]

About this time, a startling headline appeared in the *Cincinnati Commercial* over what purported to be another confession from Ellis in which he said the spirits had promised him rest and would haunt him no more, if he would tell the truth. He proceeded to claim Neal and Craft were innocent of the murder. He and two Black men whom he hired were the real murderers. On the night of the tragedy, they all went to the house of the victims and, after raping them, killed them. The Black men held the victims down while he murdered them after they had committed their hellish work. They were creeping away from the house when they suddenly came upon Neal and Craft, who were going in the direction of the house of the murdered victims. He said they hid in the bushes until these two had passed, when it occurred to him to fix the crime on them. He then left the Black men and fell in with Neal and Craft and persuaded them to go with him to a house of ill repute where some damsels of easy virtue resided. After they had been there some time, he left them on some pretext. Then he said he went to Neal's house and succeeded in stealing a coat Neal had been wearing that day. He went back to the house of the victims, smeared Neal's coat in the blood, then hid it where he thought it would be found. He said he had persuaded one of the Black men to leave the country, but the other, he said, was still in Ashland and could be produced.[130]

There are those in every part of the world who are ready to believe anything and any story, and no matter how incredible, it finds a few persons who think it true. It was so in this, but the few believers were away from Ashland and did not know anything about the surroundings. There were no bushes within hundreds of yards from the scene of the murder, and a house of ill repute did not exist in the town. This so-called confession was not given to the reporter by Ellis but by another prisoner named John Adkins who claimed Ellis had confided in him. When questioned the following day by the *Enquirer* reporter, Ellis emphatically denied making the statement to John Adkins.[131]

Detective Alf Burnett, who had a theory, took advantage of the reported confession, but as he had brought no evidence forward to sustain his supposition, no weight had been attached to it. Detective Burnett, a former publisher of West Virginia's *Advocate* and former editor of Huntington's *Advertiser*, was well acquainted with the power of the press and the influence it carried to the public.[132]

He eagerly offered his theory to an *Enquirer* correspondent:

> *Now, if you want to listen, I'll tell you just what I think of it. I was down there after the crime. I went out of pure curiosity. I was not, and am not interested or engaged, but following up clues is my business, and I followed one up then which leads me to believe that Ellis's confession is a barefaced lie; that Craft and Neal are innocent, and that three negroes are the real outragers. You must know that Ellis is a lunatic—one of those cranks who get an idea into their heads and firmly believe that certain things are just so. He said one evening to Mr. Powell that he had some evidence as to who did the deed, but not enough to make a case. A reward had been offered; the people were clamoring for the conviction of some one. You never saw anything like it; workshops and everything else stopped, and men were almost wild. A United States Marshal named Heflin heard of the remark made by Ellis and he, with a partner, worked up that story alleged to be Ellis' confession, and then got him in a room, and, pointing a revolver at him, said he would kill him if he did not confess. The result was that Ellis supplied the names of two men as innocent as you or I.*
>
> *Since that time Ellis' wife has repeatedly asked him to tell the truth, which he wildly asserts he has done. He is a deplorable looking person, and*

Alf Burnett, founder of the Eureka Detective Agency. *Public domain.*

one would readily say that he was insane. In his confession he says that he dressed before going to the door to see Craft and Neal. Why did he dress first? His wife says he did not leave the house that night. He says that Craft made him go at the mouth of a revolver, and said they were going to rape the Thomas and Gibbons girls, as they had said they would do in the fall. I contend that no one knew the girls were together that night except Mrs. Thomas and a colored family named Horten, who kept a boarding-house for railroad laborers. I have studied the alleged confession closely, and I can see several places where it doesn't hold water. Now, right here, I want to say one word about the trial, and then for my theory. Neal and Craft, who are poor, were not allowed proper defenses. They were not allowed to testify for each other or themselves. The trial was a Court-martial, in which the Judge overruled every motion for the defense. They were convicted on the slightest circumstantial evidence, and Ellis was purposely kept out, so that the defense could not impeach his testimony.

"Those are strong statements, Mr. Burnett."

I know it, but I'm sure I know what I'm talking about. Now for my theory, as there is no use in my referring to the horrors of the outrage, the killing of the girls and the boy, the fire, the excitement and arrest—all that was carefully reported by the press of the country.

About seven o'clock on the night of the 23rd, a young lady of Ashland, whom I can produce at any time, was going to her home; she met three rowdy negroes and stepped into the street to allow them to pass. One of them had an oil can, and she overheard the following: "Goin' down to Gibbons' house to steal a turkey today. Got one Thanksgivin' and three since." Mrs. Gibbons says that she had four turkeys stolen.

In the ruins was found an oil can, the spout and top melted off, but the bottom adhering and with no leak in it. Ellis said that Craft compelled him to get Mrs. Gibbons' oil can from the cupboard and pour oil on the bodies so that they would burn fast. Mrs. G. did not keep her oil can in the cupboard, and there was not a pint of oil in the house. The one that was found was larger than the one owned by Mrs. Gibbons and was brought to the house by the outragers. The evening of the 23rd an oil can was stolen from the barber shop of Willis Hockerty, a colored barber, and whose place was frequented by colored railroad hands.

The Gibbons girl came for the Thomas girl at a late hour, Mrs. Gibbons having suddenly started for Ironton. No one outside of Mrs. Thomas, except a colored family named Horten, who kept a boarding-house, knew that the Thomas girl was going to stay all night at Gibbons'. There were two Horten girls, and they were engaged to two railroad laborers. The morning after the tragedy, these two men were missing; they were known to have called on the girls the night before; While the barber, who was arrested, as he claimed to know something, saw them in Catlettsburg the morning after they left on the train going up the Big Sandy. The Horten girls said the morning after, that the two men had been gone three days. Certain it is they have never been back, and they left behind them part of their salary. I am of the opinion that they were two of the three the lady met on the street, and also that they were two of the outragers.

Captain Sents, of Charleston, formerly sheriff of Kanawha County, married Mrs. Gibbons' sister, and he left for Ashland Saturday evening. He arrived in Huntington early Sunday morning, and found he could not go any further. As he left the depot to go to the hotel he met Bill Dyerly (a negro, who formerly lived in Charleston) coming up the Ashland road. He was wet and tired, and said he was going home. Sents talked with him about the Ashland horror, and noticed that he was nervous and knew more than he cared to give away. The third morning after the horror I was informed by a Charleston lady that Bill was home, and that his mother had said that Bill knew all about the trouble. A colored agent of mine was sent to interview the old lady, and when she was asked about the Ashland trouble she said: "Jack, there's a heap sight too much been said now, and I'm afraid Bill will be arrested; he is now at Campbell's Creek."

The statement that he was at the Creek was a lie. I telegraphed and found that he had never been there. For ten days the Charleston police and my men hunted for that fellow, and at last I ran him down in a low place in the outskirts of Charleston, where he had hid for several days. He denied knowing Sentz, or having been in Ashland or Huntington, or saying anything about this crime, and contradicted himself several times. Now, I think Bill is the third party.[133]

The day after Detective Burnett's theory appeared in the newspaper, a *Courier-Journal* reporter approached Marshal Heflin to ask his thoughts on Burnett's statement. Heflin said Burnett's statement was "the most ridiculous one he had ever heard in all his experience." He continued and gave his account of what had taken place.

Mr. Powell came to me at the hotel at Ashland and informed me that he had a man in his employ whom he thought knew something about the murders. I sent for Ellis and he came to me at my room, and I had a long talk with him. After talking with him, I went out, leaving him in the room, and brought in the Citizens Committee; Mr. Campbell, Mr. Russell, and Mr. Calder. This committee had been appointed to defray all expenses that might occur in the investigation of the horrible crime. Ellis had a talk with them and gave them to understand that he knew something about the affair. I did not arrest him at that time and let him go home. But because the excitement was so great amongst the populace, I was afraid the mill hands would mob him if they found out that he was implicated, so I went out and brought him in again about seven o'clock. And while I was out arresting Neal and Craft, he made his confession, as published to Mr. Campbell, cashier of the National Bank of Ashland. His confession was made before three of the first citizens of Ashland.

I did not know anything about his confession until I returned after arresting Neal and Craft. And right here I wish to say in regard to Ellis' being forced to confess at the point of a pistol, it is a lie and I deny it most emphatically; and a damn'd lie at that! The confession had been made in my absence. And as far as nobody knowing that Miss Thomas went to Mrs. Gibbons' until late at night; that is another lie.

In regard to the negroes, that was a scheme I fixed up to draw Mr. Burnett off into the mountains. My reason for doing this was that Burnett was monkeying around there and getting in the way. I wanted to get him out of my way so I could work the case without having him nosing around. When I put him on the negro scheme, he went to West Virginia and tried to make a case out on the three negroes, I suppose. They had worked on the railroad near Ashland, and I knew that they had left there three weeks before the murders, because I had traced them to Huntington,

> *WV and found out that they had been away from the scene of the tragedy for about three weeks.*
>
> *Burnett, so the paper says, thinks George Ellis is a crank and insane. But I know one thing; if I was out looking for fools, cranks or lunatics, and was to meet Ellis and Burnett on the road, I would certainly take Burnett to be the man I was looking for. Burnett tried to draw $9.50 from the Committee on the strength of the negro scheme and I told the Committee not to pay it. I suppose that is what's the matter with him.*[134]

About a week after this, it was reported that Ellis had made yet another confession. This time it was reported Ellis claimed he knew nothing of the murders—and that not only were Neal and Craft innocent, but he had nothing to do with the murders either. He said he was forced to make his initial confession under threats from Marshal Heflin and A.C. Campbell. He said he could not remember talking to his wife when he told her Neal and Craft were guilty and could not remember what he had said on the witness stand during the trials. In reporting this confession by Ellis, the correspondent stated that at the Lexington jail Neal and Craft had found means of communication with Ellis. The reporter also admitted this confession was only obtained after much persuasion and when the reporter had been himself in jail and locked up as a prisoner for a week.[135]

In response to this, Marshal Heflin visited the jail in Lexington and obtained an interview with Ellis, which is given here in his own words:

> *I arrived in this city at two o'clock today* [February 24] *and went at once to the jail to see George Ellis with regard to his alleged confession in yesterday's* Enquirer. *I went into his cell in company with the jailer, and asked him if he had made these statements, he answered me vehemently, "I did not." Was what you said at Catlettsburg the truth? "Yes, it was. People have been here trying to get me to make other statements, but I didn't." I also asked the jailer if an* Enquirer *reporter had been confined in the cell with Ellis for a week to get this confession, and he said, "No sir." The jailer said to Ellis, "If you've not told the truth, why don't you tell it?" and Ellis answered, "I have told the truth." The fact that the* Enquirer *representative in this city has willfully lied is very evident. I thought the* Enquirer *had sensation sufficient from Ashland, over the signature of John T. Norris, and from Charleston, W.Va., over the signature of Alf Burnett, to not jump at such reports. With regard to Ellis's confession, I was not present when Ellis made his confession. I had arrested him and*

> *put him in the hands of the Citizens Committee and gone after Neal and Craft. And while I was gone he made his confession to Mr. Campbell and others, of which I knew nothing until I had returned with Craft and Neal, and was told of it by Mr. Campbell. I was a sworn witness in the trial, and never heard Ellis make any statement under oath. I cautioned Ellis in regard to implicating Neal and Craft in the presence of the Committee, but he insisted that they were the guilty parties.*[136]

Having an accusing finger pointed at him did not set well with A.C. Campbell either, as he was compelled to respond to this latest and different version of Ellis's confession as well as Alf Burnett's accusations. About Ellis's original confession, Campbell said the following:

> *We told him we wanted only the truth. There were no threats made by anyone, no pistols or knives exhibited by anyone. I was with them until they were landed in jail. No harshness was used. Marshal Heflin was kind enough to take off his overcoat and put it on Ellis, who was thinly clad. I do not believe that George Ellis made the so-called second and third confessions. If he had done so, he would certainly have told one truth. It is somewhat remarkable that every variation from his original statement has been reported from some jailbird. The people of Boyd County are satisfied that the right men are convicted. They would be sorry to have any more innocent blood shed.*[137]

What the motives were for these contradictory statements it would be difficult to say, but the supposition prevailing at the time was that they were drawn out through influences brought to bear by friends of Neal and Craft, who had hoped to profit by the feeling the confessions would incite in people. And it seemed to be working, at least in that part of the state, for by then, the belief in Neal and Craft's innocence was steadily gaining ground.[138]

In the meantime, the Circuit Court's decision was appealed, and the session of the Court of Appeals commenced on April 10, just four days before the day fixed for the execution. It was understood their case was first on the docket, it being by far the most important one. No one doubted that its merits would be speedily looked into, and the people waited. The time rolled on, and the tenth was at hand. Every avenue of intelligence was watched with great interest. The time for the execution arrived, but a writ of supersedeas had been filed in the court that suspended the executions of Neal and Craft, and the month of April rolled away to be followed by May.[139]

The Ashland Tragedy

On May 22, Craft and Neal, with several other prisoners, attempted to escape. They made a ladder from the blankets of their beds by tearing them into strips and plaiting them together, but the attempt was discovered and frustrated. Still the court had not acted, and a terrible feeling was brewing—a feeling that would have made the guilty prisoners tremble. The emotion would swell to such proportions that men who loved the law would be impelled by it to forget all restraint and substitute for the slow, tiresome ponderings of judges the vengeance (swift and sure) of an outraged people.[140]

10

GEORGE ELLIS

George Ellis was brought back from Lexington looking exceedingly well and was arraigned for trial on Tuesday, May 30. He was brought into court, accompanied by his wife, who, throughout the entire trial, sat beside him and frequently manifested considerable emotion. Ellis kept a handkerchief to his eyes and seemed to display much feeling. The prosecution made a specific charge against him, that of killing Robbie Gibbons, and tried him for this crime. The jury consisted of the following gentlemen: Wyatt L. Clay, Thomas B. Davis, Gabe Riffe, William F. Layne, George B. Johnston, James Williams, W.T. Moore, John Klaiber, G.B. Norton, E.M.K. Hanley, John M. Clay and James Barber.[141]

The evidence was, with a few exceptions (which are given here as reported by editor Huff), a repetition of the evidence in the case of William Neal. A.C. Campbell was questioned in regard to a report that circulated about his using a pistol to extort a confession from Ellis, and this was proven false by his testimony.

Roland C. Burns said his understanding of the former testimony was Craft brought the ax into the room but Ellis carried it out.

The next witness, Obe Gallaher said,

> *I was in the employ of the Scioto Valley Railroad at the time of the murder. On the morning of the murder, about 3 o'clock, a man wearing a light hat and I think light clothes, asked me about the trains leaving; I*

The Ashland Tragedy

George Ellis confessed to the murders of the Gibbons children and the Carico girl. *Public domain, courtesy of the Boyd County Public Library.*

told him it was gone and there would be no more leaving until 9 o'clock. I did not know who the man was, and never saw him after until I saw him in the courthouse, and I think Ellis is the man.

J.C. Miller testified,

I had known Ellis four or five months before the murder; I was up to the burned house about 8 o'clock the morning of the fire. I met Ellis on the upper side of the house coming from the railroad. I spoke to him and said it is strange that this is burned, and the lives of these children lost, so close to you all, and you know nothing about it. He answered yes, and said he got up about 3 o'clock and went to the brickyard and made a fire. He said he then came back home and made a fire. From Ellis' house to the lower end of town it is about one and one-fourth miles.

William Carroll said,

I was at Geiger's addition Christmas day. My wife was at Mr. Simmons'. I saw George Ellis at the burned house Sunday after the murder. We talked about the murder. Ellis said he suspicioned who it was that did it, and said he thought it was Ellis Craft and a married man but did not say who the married man was. I saw him after that in a field above the brickyard. He walked up the branch that ran through the field, and then down again. I saw him afterward near Geiger, Powell & Ferguson's store, when he said about the same things to me that he had said, about suspecting Ellis Craft and a married man. I afterward saw him on

Winchester street, in Ashland and as we were walking down the street he said, "If you will be a friend to me, I will tell you how you can get that reward." This was the morning before the arrest. Ellis was working at the furnace and I have known him about twelve months. His character was good so far as I know.

Henry J. Kelly said,

I was one of the guards to Craft, Neal and Ellis when they were taken to Maysville; we started from here on the ferryboat, and were pursued by the Mountain Girl, *a larger and faster boat than the ferryboat. The Mountain Girl was gaining upon us. There were a great many men on the pursuing boat. They seemed very much excited, and I thought we would be overtaken. Neal asked me if he could talk to Ellis, and I said I don't think you have got very long to live, and I guess we might as well let you talk as not. Neal said, "Ellis, how could you give me away like this and ruin my wife and little children—but if they hang me, they will hang an innocent man." Ellis then said to them, "Boys, you know we were there—I would not tell a lie and meet my God for 10,000 worlds."*

Attorney Thomas Brown took the stand:

I know George Ellis. I saw him in the jail at Lexington. He said he had made a statement to D.K. Weis, and seemed disinclined to talk to me, but I insisted that I had come out there to see him and was an attorney in the other cases. He then made a statement in which he said that all other statements were false, and that he and the others were innocent. He said that Campbell and Heflin pointed pistols at him in the hotel when he made his confession, and again when they visited him in the jail at Catlettsburg. He said they did not meet at the cemetery, but at that time he was over at the furnace, and he could prove it by Cyrus Wilson, Wilson Miller and another man whom he thought was an engineer. He said he had worked in the coke ovens in Virginia, and that his physician had told him if he did not leave, he would lose his mind. I was induced to go to Lexington by a letter to which George Ellis' name was affixed. The letter was written in a very good business hand and with different ink. The substance of the letter was that he had something to communicate.

The Ashland Tragedy

Samuel S. Savage said,

> *I know George Ellis. I came to Catlettsburg in the hack with Ellis when he was first arrested and he said to me, "Judge, you should have known I was guilty when you saw me up at Geiger's addition." He said this in the hack between Ashland and Catlettsburg. He did not seem excited. I was not asked about this when on the stand in the Craft and Neal trials. Ellis was not threatened or coerced into saying anything to me.*

Marshal James Heflin testified, "I was not in Maysville when George Ellis was confined in that jail. I was at Lexington about the middle of last February and I saw Ellis in jail. He complained of being annoyed by visitors, and said he was sick, but looked as well as ever to me."

This ended the testimony in one of the worst cases on record: a man on trial accused of being accessory to the worst crimes imaginable—rape, murder and house burning—and without any excuse save that he was forced to do what he did. The case was given to the jury Thursday morning, June 2, 1882 at eleven o'clock.[142]

The jury's deliberation lasted twenty-two hours. They brought in a verdict of guilty and fixed the penalty at imprisonment for life. It was said that eleven of the jurors were for hanging, but one held out until the others were finally brought around to the verdict given. The verdict was not so well received as it might have been by those interested, but it was thought that all would be allowed to pass in view of the fact that Ellis's guiltier companions would receive the extreme penalty.[143]

The next dreadful act of this drama is described by editor Huff, except where noted.

Between 11 and 12 o'clock Friday night, when a hush, a solemn stillness had settled down upon our city; when the silence of the midnight had succeeded the confusion of the day, dreamy silence, only broken by the rumble of the ponderous machinery at either furnace—one at each extreme of the town—but, listen! Tramp, tramp? What can this be? We listen—up Front Street toward the furnace. We count one, two, three, and on up to eighteen—eighteen men with black masks on, through which eighteen pairs of eyes gleaned with a determined light, not to be mistaken.

Something was to be done! Some act that required resolution and will! Some act of retributive justice! The firm tread, the orderly bearing, spoke of discipline and power. The black watchman, Albert Ingram, who was also a fireman on the Charraroi, sat gazing skyward and lost in thought when he was aroused. He listened and sprang up, and, casting an anxious glance around, found he and his engine were surrounded. The men moved with the precision and regularity of military veterans, and the leader gave orders to numbers, not to names. Albert sprang to the ground and attempted to fly, but it was too late, and at the stern command of the leader of this mysterious band, he stopped. And, with trembling frame he climbed back on to the engine. He was ordered to fire up and he hastened to obey.[144]

The fire under the boiler was already warm, and soon the hissing steam told of readiness. One of the masks then grasped the throttle, and with a flat car attached, upon which the grim and silent company were sitting in various attitudes, the locomotive started, and like a monster of darkness, moved away softly, silently!

Ashland was left behind, and the sleep of her citizens had not been disturbed. Field, orchard and forest were left behind. The junction of the Chattaroi and depot was soon reached, but the switch was wrong and there was no key. This did not check the determined crew; a pick supplied the place of a key and the lock yielded! The rails sprang into place and the journey continued. The wheels revolved so silently that the birds in the woods were not awakened, and the towering hills found no sound to echo.

The speed was increased. They glided into Catlettsburg, and on through her silent streets to the very center of the town, to where the shadows of the temple of justice could be seen and felt, and where the jail, outlined against the sky, looked gloomy, silent and forbidding, holding within its walls and grated windows and iron doors, a cowering, shivering human being—a man who had been tried for murder and found guilty—sat waiting. A dark foreboding, a premonition of coming doom kept him awake; an indescribable something caused him to arise and dress, and, seated on his prison couch, he awaited the footsteps of the avengers.

Could we look into the shadowy depths of his beating heart? Could we read the thoughts that in wild confusion chased each other through his throbbing brain? We could paint a picture of ruined hopes and a blasted life that would touch the hardest heart. The dim lights in the corridor of the jail cast fanciful shadows on the stone floor, and stillness reigned. A knock was heard, softly at first, then firm and loud. The jailer, aroused from slumber, asked, "Who's there?"

"Open the door!" came in measured tones from the outside.

"I will not open the door," answered the jailer.

Then followed a moment of suspense and a crash! One of the windows was broken in, and the jailer, seeing that an entrance could not be prevented, opened the door, and the masked men filed in. A demand for the keys was promptly refused by the watchful guardian of the prison, but a glance at the flashing eyes showed the folly of resistance, and from the pockets of his night clothes he produced them. The leader took the keys and as he was followed by six of the men, he repaired to the cell with admonition to the other prisoners to keep quiet, delivered in a tone not to be misconstrued. They went straight to the cot and found the murderer, ready. He offered no resistance, but with one grim guard on either side, two in the rear and two in the front, they proceeded to the open air. The jail was locked, the keys returned to the proper authorities, and the avengers, with puffing engine, were returning.

The murderer, seated on the floor of the car, surrounded by the silent masks, uttered not a word. The return was quick, but faster fly the thoughts of the wretched man whose life would soon go out to pay the forfeit, to satisfy the feeling his act had aroused. They were then in sight of the place where, but a few short months ago, the charred and mangled remains of the children had been taken from the burning building. The murderer was cool and collected, and had evidently made up his mind to die, and calmly awaited the final issue.

They came to a stand-still just in the rear of the scene of the tragedy and alighted and went over into the brickyard that has figured so conspicuously in the evidence and halted under a sycamore tree. George Ellis was asked if he had anything to say, and he answered, "Nothing. The statement I made in court was true; the other two are guilty, and so am I; not of actual murder, but of enough. I deserve to die." He was then asked if he wanted to pray, to which he replied, "No, I have made all the preparation I can, and am ready."

He was then pulled up from the ground and allowed to hang for a moment, then let down, considerably choked, but still alive. When he had sufficiently recovered, he said: "Oh! Why didn't you let me hang?"

He was asked, "Is there anything you have not told?"

He answered: "No; let me hang this time." But one last request was made by Ellis when he asked that his body not be mutilated. He was then hauled up, and the rope secured. He died without a struggle; with his life he paid the penalty. And thus, closed the last chapter in the life of George Ellis, a poor, confused and tormented soul.[145]

The moon peeped in and out behind the clouds and the shadows swallowed up the retreating forms of the avenging band as the engine ran silently back to its accustomed place, and all was quiet.

The tree on which George Ellis was hanged is a sycamore, within one hundred yards of the burned house; between the house and brickyard, in a smooth, green part of the pasture. On the same tree and same limb had been fastened a swing, where the children had played, and where many a happy hour had been spent by them, no doubt watched by the very men who afterward became their murderers.

The body as it hung in the morning was dressed in a black coat and pants. The boots looked as though they had traveled through mud and water. A hat lay on the ground and a black cap partially covered his face. His hands had been tied behind him with a dark green piece of cotton goods. His face was turned up and pale, not black, as would be expected. His feet were eighteen inches from the ground. He looked as natural as though he had died without a struggle. The crowd commenced to gather about the spot early in the morning, and during the forenoon the population of Ashland had mostly been out; men, women and children, with very few exceptions, seemed to be as unconcerned as though nothing unusual had happened.[146]

Ellis was placed in a coffin, and a grave was dug in the nearby cemetery. But around the noon hour, just before he was buried, his father appeared from near Ceredo, West Virginia, in a two-horse wagon. He claimed the body, and it was delivered to him.[147]

As much as the good citizens of Ashland had tried and hoped to avoid the distinction of "mob rule town," it was now too late. In the eyes of those afar, the lynching of Ellis had branded Ashland as a vengeful, barbarous and unrestrained community. But many questions demanded answers.

Who were the masked murderers? None could identify them, not the Chattaroi fireman, nor the Catlettsburg jailer. Speculation raced through the minds of the people. Could it have been a mob composed of local citizens whose patience had expired partially due to the passivity of the courts? Could it have been a roving band of murderous Kentucky Regulators whose proclamation asserted to protect honest and honorable people, while threatening murderers with lynch law? The action against Ellis was strikingly similar to that which was wrought against John Wagoner just five months previous in Ironton, Ohio.[148]

Could it have been friends of the two convicted murderers, who may have hoped that with the death of Ellis, his original confession would now have also been dead and buried, and of no avail against them? And perhaps the Court of Appeals would now finally act and grant them both new trials? No one had more to gain by the death of George Ellis than Craft and Neal.

Where were the soldiers? Why was Ellis not protected the same as Craft and Neal? Why did Judge Brown and Governor Blackburn think it unnecessary to cradle Ellis in the safety of the troops? By offering his confession, George Ellis thought he was "turning state's evidence." But by all accounts, he had presented himself as a rat, a squealer, a sneak, an informant. And nobody likes a snitch. In the minds of the people, from jailbirds to jurors, and everyone in between, George Ellis was a low-life stool pigeon. Fascinating as it is, by his confession, Ellis was thought less of than the rapists, arsonists and murderers—Craft and Neal. Ellis had wrestled with his conscience for more than a week, knowing that by confessing he would become the scourge of society. But he could bear the burden no longer. His was a dilemma of the nth degree—live with what he had seen and done or relieve his conscience and face the consequences. He chose the latter. But apparently Governor Blackburn's edict to "support the dignity of the law by protecting the prisoners" did not apply to the stool pigeon, Ellis. With no troops or extra guards sent to protect him, he was intentionally left alone in Catlettsburg, as bait for any mob willing to do the dirty work. The blood of George Ellis must be, at least partially, laid at the feet of Judge Brown and Governor Blackburn for failing to provide adequate protection for Ellis as they had found necessary for Craft and Neal.

When the news of the Ellis lynching was taken to Neal and Craft in Lexington, Craft said it was regretful, but he and Neal reaffirmed their innocence in the whole matter. Both prisoners continued to greet numerous daily visitors and their fame and the belief in their innocence continued to grow.[149]

The popularity and following they had received soon rivaled that of the assassin, Charles Guiteau, who while incarcerated, had been gaining ten to forty dollars per day selling autographs and photographs of himself. The fascination and adoration shown to convicted killers by large numbers of seemingly rational and intelligent people is quite remarkable.[150]

11

NEW TRIALS

Emma Carico and the two Gibbons children were at rest, and their destroyers were to be punished—so thought the people. But days had lengthened into months, and the dreaded expectation was realized when the Court of Appeals reversed the decisions of the lower court on a technicality of the law—not that one of the judges thought from the testimony the prisoners were innocent, but because Judge Brown had failed in his instructions to the jury to say a verdict could not be found on the testimony of an accomplice, unless supported by sufficient corroborative evidence. The opinion of the court was delivered by Judge Hines, and it follows here in substance:

Appellant (Craft/Neal) was indicted on the charge of murder, tried, convicted and sentenced to death. The conviction appears to have been had principally upon the evidence of an accomplice, and the only question we need consider, precluding no other, is whether the court properly instructed the jury. Sections 241 and 242 of the Criminal Code are as follows:

"A conviction cannot be had upon the testimony of an accomplice unless corroborated by other evidence to connect the defendant with the commission of the offence: and the corroboration is not sufficient if it merely shows that the offence was committed, and the circumstances thereof. In all cases whereby law two witnesses or one witness with corroborating circumstances are requisite to warrant a conviction, if the requisition be not fulfilled,

the court shall instruct the jury to render a verdict of acquittal by which instruction they are bound."

The failure to instruct as indicated was clearly error which under the circumstances of this case was necessarily prejudicial to appellant(s). The jury should have been instructed in the language, substantially, of Section 241. For the reasons assigned in the opinion, the judgment of conviction is reversed, and cause remanded with direction for a new trial.[151]

In his attempt to save face, Judge Brown told a reporter that the Court of Appeals had, in fact, affirmed his instructions but had sent the case back for another trial because the judgment rendered by the jury was not supported by the facts. Clearly, Judge Brown was either confused by the higher court's ruling and did not understand it, or he simply lied to the reporter.[152]

Respect for Judge Brown was rapidly decaying among the citizens of Boyd County. His prior refusal to accept the citizens' pledge to protect the prisoners in lieu of the governor's State Guard left many folks confused and angry. But his error to properly instruct the juries that lead to the higher court's reversal of convictions infuriated the people. All the work, time and effort spent by the attorneys, the jurors and the witnesses who had performed their duties in the first trials so judiciously were brought to naught because of his error. Up until now, Judge Brown had been considered one of the most able and impartial judges to have sat on the bench. But his actions in this notorious case had left some wondering if his Southern sympathies had marred his judgment against a people who had largely remained loyal to the Union during, and after, the Civil War.[153]

With new trials granted by the Court of Appeals, Craft and Neal now had a second chance for acquittal, much to the chagrin of the Ashland people who believed they had been rightly convicted the first time. A rumor had reached the ears of Judge Brown that his life was now in danger, so he had quietly slipped out of Catlettsburg to Frankfort, where he stayed for a few days, thinking the people, in time, would cool off. While there was a high level of indignation at Ashland against Judge Brown, there was no organized movement against him.[154]

The public pulse was aroused to action by the announcement that the next (Craft and Neal) trials were set for the third day of the October term of the Boyd Circuit Court, and the memories of that fatal night at Ashland were stirred. And now, in the autumn of another year, when the leaves—beautifully colored by the near approach of the frost king—trembled nervously and with each gentle, whispering wind fluttered with a sigh to the ground. Sad hearts remembered how the gorgeous tints of autumn once sent the thrilling notes of bright childhood's laughter echoing among the glorious hills as the happy children gathered the brown nuts and beautiful leaves. But the grave, cold and relentless, had gathered the loved ones. And the murderers, stained with the blood of the innocents, from behind prison walls embraced the darkened hope that their convictions might be overturned—now that George Ellis had been removed from the whole horrible picture. Their friends in the outer world were alert and watchful and had taken advantage of every ebb and flow of the tide of public feeling. The adjacent counties had been canvassed for evidence to present to the court in the trial for change of venue, and the affidavits of a score of individuals had been secured. All the ingenuity and cunning of the lawyers for the defense had been employed, and upon the moldering ashes of excitement past, they had anchored a foundation for new life and hope for the murderers.[155]

The twenty-third day of October came, and the Circuit Court, destined never to be forgotten, destined to be seared upon the hearts of hundreds of law-abiding citizens and its memory indelibly written in blood upon the fateful history of Boyd County, convened. The slow, monotonous drag of court proceedings was the order of the first three days, and then life and interest were injected when the judge pronounced the names of Craft and Neal.[156]

All sprang forward to listen. The case was called, and an order made to return them to Boyd County in custody of the sheriff. The order did not embrace a request to the governor to send soldiers to guard the prisoners, but a private communication from Judge Brown and numerous affidavits sent by the friends of the prisoners were considered by the governor sufficient grounds to send five companies of state militia with one piece of artillery as guards. In sending the troops to Catlettsburg, Governor Blackburn had stated they were sent "to support the dignity of the law, if the whole county of Boyd had to be killed in protecting the prisoners."[157]

A brief glimpse of Luke Blackburn's tenure as governor of Kentucky is necessary and given here:

> *Governor Blackburn, a physician, came to office amid controversy and remained mired in strife throughout his term. His work during an 1878 yellow fever epidemic in Kentucky earned him the appellation of "Hero of Hickman" and won him the gubernatorial election. Most of his work as governor focused on a single issue—prison reform. With no parole system in place, the only way a prisoner could be released prior to [a] full sentence was to die, or to be pardoned by the governor. His decision to relieve overcrowding*

in prisons by pardon earned him the nickname, "Lenient Luke." By the time his term had ended he had pardoned more than a thousand prisoners, including nearly four hundred Regulators. Such actions angered many. By the conclusion of his term as governor, Blackburn had almost no allies. He was shouted down and booed by his own party as he sought to defend his record. The press ignored most of his minor achievements and instead wrote about the pardon record of the man whom one paper called "the old imbecile."[158]

During the Civil War, this governor had engaged in germ warfare against civilians in the North. Blackburn served as the civilian aide-de-camp of Confederate general Sterling Price for a period during the war. In April 1864, Blackburn, believing at the time the disease was infectious and easily spread, initiated a plot and shipped clothing and bedding from yellow fever victims to certain locations in the North to cripple the Union's war effort. A New Bern (one of Blackburn's targets) newspaper commented on his plot after learning the city had been targeted: "This hideous and long studied plan to deliberately murder innocent men, women and children, who had never wronged him in any manner, is regarded here as an act of cruelty without a parallel."[159]

The political, cultural and geographical divisions that significantly identified Kentucky during the Civil War continued to linger and fester long after the conclusion of the armed conflict. While it is considered commendable for a governor to support the dignity of the law, it is surprising to hear the sitting governor of a state to declare open season on its citizens: in this case, the people of Boyd County. The governor had apparently used mob rumors as a pretext to declare war on Boyd County. And when war is declared, murder becomes sanctioned by decree with no legal ramifications. In his defense of the two convicted murderers (of the most monstrous crimes known in this section), Blackburn's Herod-like proclamation to kill all the men, women and children of Boyd County served only to stoke the smoldering ashes of frustration and agitation among the citizens of Boyd County. And as a result, an effigy of the governor was hung on the same sycamore tree that witnessed the dying breath of George Ellis.[160]

In writing this history, it is not our purpose to enter into a discussion of the rights or wrongs of official action in this matter, but knowing as we do the deep feeling that prevailed in Boyd County upon this one subject, we cannot refrain from saying the ingress of these guards was mortifying in the extreme to the best people interested. And to all who did not directly sympathize with the murderers it was exasperating and maddening. Here were the men who had been tried by juries composed of men of unquestioned honor and ability, and who, through the weary, dragging trials, heard with patience all the evidence, giving proper weight to each circumstance, and importance to every word of testimony. And with every inclination given to the side of mercy, but the verdict was guilty! And justice—inflexible justice—smiled its approval.[161]

But here were these men escorted by a guard—armed strangers, who seemed to handle their guns with nervous anxiety, and their every action indicated a desire to try their new weapons. One of them, Private John Hurley of the Emmet Rifles, clumsily shot himself in the leg, whereby an order was issued by their commander, forbidding any private to carry a pistol. But Catlettsburg, the county seat, was transformed. The tramp of armed men was heard night and day.[162]

Craft and Neal were quartered in an upstairs room of the courthouse. People from the surrounding towns and country came flocking in, and the town was alive. John Gibbons was not permitted in the courtroom. Judge Brown had prohibited the old man's presence in response to a rumor Gibbons had planned to shoot both Craft and Neal in the open courtroom.[163]

If there was any truth behind that rumor, who could blame Gibbons for surrendering his feelings to a vengeful wrath? His baby girl had been raped, viciously murdered, then set on fire. His one-legged, energetic son's life was snuffed out while attempting to prevent the hellish work of the fiends, who viewed the lives of his children disposable, meaningless. Who could blame Gibbons for the boiling rise of retribution that must have flowed through his veins just for the chance of five minutes alone with the county's most notorious criminal and his shameful accomplice? Those two, who went to the Gibbons humble home that fateful night to "have some fun" and had since become bizarre media celebrities, were sickening to look upon. It would seem likely the thought of the events that transpired that night continually replayed in the mind of Gibbons. And those two heathens lurked in the shadows, while the whole country had hated and hunted for Gibbons and would have stood silently by and watched him hang for a crime he did not commit, had it not been for the intervention of Marshal Heflin. Who could blame Gibbons for wanting to shoot them?

The prisoners were brought into court, and amid breathless silence, the application for a change of venue was presented. We will not give the names of the witnesses who testified. Most of them were good men. Several of the best citizens testified their belief the prisoners could have a fair trial in Boyd County. The judge, however, ruled against this opinion, granted the change of venue and fixed Carter County as the one for the new trial. We will not try to explain the feeling that took possession of the people. Some were frenzied with excitement, others calm in the consciousness of their own utter helplessness. The time for the new hearing was set for the February term of the Circuit Court. The delay was sickening. The prisoners were to be taken back to Lexington, and a few hot-headed young men and boys (who represented the feeling of the cooler people, but not the sense) determined to prevent the guards from doing this, and many wild plans were suggested and discarded.[164]

12
RIVER MASSACRE

The day for the prisoners' departure had arrived. The soldiers had come by rail, but they abandoned the idea of returning by that mode, and the river was selected. The *Granite State*, a commodious steamboat commanded by Captain William Kirker, was pressed into the service, and the guards marched their prisoners to the wharf boat. All were about to embark when a train of cars from Ashland steamed into the town, bearing about two hundred men and boys.

Major John R. Allen, who was described as a young, beardless lawyer from Lexington—highly excitable, and wholly unfit for the duties assigned him—immediately formed one company of his men on the Catlettsburg Main Street, facing the so-called mob. Another company was stationed at the foot of Division Street and another in a vacant lot on Main, thus completely commanding the position. The soldiers, 215 in number, were composed of the following seven companies and their captains: McCreary Guards, Captain J. Lampton Price; Lexington Guards, Captain D. Vertner Johnson; Emmet Rifles, Captain E.W. Fitzgerald; Blackburn Guards, Captain Thomas F. Hughes; Company C, First Regiment, Captain D.F.C. Weller; Nuckols Guards, Captain Joe L. Rodman; First Section Louisville Light Artillery, Lieutenant C.B. Bly.[165]

They were armed with the latest improved army rifles. The boys from Ashland had perhaps forty old shotguns and pistols. Three or four gentlemen who had gone up on the train (more for the purpose of keeping the rash boys out of danger than anything else) now advanced and demanded the surrender of the prisoners. This Major Allen refused, but he conceded that the few men who had demanded the prisoners were sober, discreet, law-abiding citizens, and they even shook hands when they departed.[166]

The major said, however, that he and his men would fight to the last rather than give up the murderers, which meant that the lives of hundreds of persons would be sacrificed to protect two of the worst criminals on record—but we do not purpose to give vent to any feeling, choosing rather to give facts and await judgment from the people. The leaders of the crowd on the train finally prevailed upon the others to abandon the hope of getting the prisoners, and the train prepared to return to Ashland. In the meantime, the soldiers had fallen back to the boat, dragging the cannon with them, and when all were on board, the steamer backed from the wharf and started down the river, bearing the murderers, and those who were so soon to be murderers, toward Ashland—fated Ashland.[167]

The events that followed can best be described as one of the darkest hours in the history of Kentucky, and except where noted are given here by editor Huff.

A telegram was received at Ashland from Catlettsburg that the guards and prisoners had left on the *Granite State* and would soon pass Ashland. This news spread, and in a short time a number of citizens gathered on Front Street and along the bank of the river to see the soldiers and their charge go by, little thinking what the result would be. The crowd was composed mostly of women and children. Soon after the boat left Catlettsburg the train returned with its load, arriving at Ashland a few minutes ahead of the boat.

Most of the crowd exited the train cars, scattering in different directions. Some went down Front street, some toward the river, and a few to the ferry boat (although they had been admonished not to go). The *Granite State* came in sight. The life-preservers and other movable articles on the boat had been piled around the guards. Behind these were the latent missiles of death, only waiting the touch of the finger to do the deadly work. And while the men, women and children of Ashland stood on the grade, bank, street and in their homes, unprotected from as much as a birdshot, the boys in uniform were concealed from sight and danger. Major Allen stood ready to give the order to fire if he felt it necessary. The sheriff, under whose order the soldiers should have been, was safe in the ladies' cabin, while Craft and Neal were lying flat on the cabin floor, where no danger could have reached them.

About eighteen men and boys, two-thirds of whom were boys from twelve to eighteen years of age, boarded the ferryboat and ordered the pilot,

William Kouns, to move out. And as the little ferry advanced slowly toward the *Granite State*, the people on the shore stood amazed. The ferryboat hailed the *Granite State*, but no answer came. The boats were then about three hundred yards apart. For a moment silence reigned. Not a sound was heard except the wheels of the boats and would that we could stop here—but no—a sound was heard as a shot from a small pistol, which was followed by another. And then, quicker than it could be told, came a volley from the *Granite State*, which disabled the ferry and silenced all other shooting.

Everyone on the ferry sought shelter wherever he could find it. If the firing had ceased then, the soldiers might have gone home with a feeling that they had acted only in self-defense, but the firing did not cease. In his official report to Adjutant General Nuckols, Major Allen wrote that he had "two-hundred unexperienced marksmen shooting at the ferry…and it was not surprising that a great number of shots directed at the ferry should have missed their mark and carried death into the crowd on the shore."[168]

Volley after volley came from the soldiers' guns until nearly 1,500 shots were fired—not at the ferryboat—but at the men, women and children on the grade, on the bank, on the streets, in the houses, and in the depot, away below the ferry, and, in fact, in every direction where human beings could be seen, of any size or sex. In every direction the people fell—some dead, others mortally wounded and some slightly wounded. The *Granite State* had gotten far down the river, and the firing had finally ceased.

The greatest excitement prevailed. People were running in every direction in search of loved ones. Among the first to fall and register the dark crime of murder against the soldiers of Kentucky was L.W. Reppert—shot through the heart. Reppert was an aged and respected citizen who occupied a position on the top of the riverbank. He had been one of the most active in trying to keep the crowd from going on the ferry and little dreamed that death was near at hand.

The next was George Keener, a young man, brave, noble and generous, well known and loved by all. The cruel bullet could not have found a dearer mark. He left a young wife and little baby to mourn his untimely end. The cries of the wounded filled the air. John Baugh, shot in the shoulder; Robert Prichard, shot in the mouth; Martin Dunlap, aged fourteen years, shot in the right hip; Martin Greer, shot in the knee joint later died from his wound; Will Springer, a promising young man, had his shoulder shattered; Robert Lother, shot through the abdomen. James McDonald, a brother-in-law of the two murdered Gibbons children, was shot three times and later died.[169]

Willie Serey, aged fourteen, an interesting boy, was shot in the knee. He was on the river grade when he fell. A man ran by, and little Willie said, "Please, Mister, take me up, won't you? I'm shot and can't walk." But the man replied roughly and ran on. Jacob Hall came by and Willie appealed to him, and the rough, strong man bowed over the pale boy, whose lifeblood was flowing upon the cindered bank, and said: "I cannot carry you my son, but I will lie down by you and they can't shoot you again, my boy." And he did. The balls were flying in all directions all around them, but this noble man placed his form between the leaden messengers of death and the poor boy. Little Willie is dead now, but his friends will not soon forget the man who braved danger to help him.[170]

Julius Sohmer was shot in the leg. Mrs. Jackson Serey, a young married lady, who had left her child just two months old at home in bed, was shot in the shoulder and breast. Next came Charley Bollinger, a bright schoolboy, who was shot in the leg and terribly wounded. Mrs. H.B. Butler, who occupied a position in the second story of the depot at the lower part of town, was very badly wounded. Alexander Harris was frightfully wounded in the thigh, and after lingering in great pain for two days, died. Eighteen months before, he had led to the altar a beautiful bride, and fortune seemed to smile kindly upon them. But now, with a little child in her arms, the heartbroken widow waters with tears the grave of one of the noblest young men of our state. Graham Randal was shot through the shoulder. John Gallagher was shot in the hip. Quite a number of others were slightly wounded. A horse was shot under Frank Butler in the city, and another horse was killed near the mayor's office. A cow, a half mile away at the Ashland park, was also killed by a shot from the boat.[171]

The *Granite State* had passed around the bend and out of sight. Two soldiers were slightly scratched by the impotent weapons in the hands of the boys on the ferry. Sadness and silence settled down upon our little city; noted for her hospitality and kindness to all. Her background of hills had echoed the cries of her dead and dying, and the trees had waved with their arms of green in the thundering sound of gunshots that crushed the heartstrings of her citizens. One volley from the military would have been sufficient to silence the crew on the ferryboat. Yet when they opened fire on the people upon the riverbank, they themselves had descended to the level of a mob. The soldiers went on their way rejoicing, while the people of Ashland mourned over their dead and wounded.[172]

We give first the official report of Major Allen, commander of the troops on board the *Granite State*:

The Ashland Tragedy

To Gov. L.P. Blackburn: At 12 o'clock p.m. on November 1st, our command marched to the river front at Catlettsburg to wait the arrival of a boat to convey us home. We marched the prisoners, Neal and Craft, with two companies as guards into the wharf-boat and left the remaining companies at the top of the hill to repulse an attack which we anticipated from the Ashland mob. A few minutes after we took our position a train of cars, consisting of one locomotive, one passenger and five flat cars, closely packed with a mob from Ashland, Ky, arrived. A delegation from the mob waited on me and demanded the prisoners, Neal and Craft, threatening that if we did not surrender them peaceably, they would use force. Their demand was peremptorily refused. They then informed us that they would attack us as our boat passed Ashland with a force of at least 2000 men, supported by a ferryboat with a battery of four pieces of artillery. We then withdrew to our boat, the Granite State, *and started down the river. The mob at the same time took their train and headed toward Ashland. The train ran along the riverbank about a mile at the same speed as our boat, and just before leaving the river opened fire on us. But our troops, with great coolness and self-restraint, did not fire, although the bullets of the mob struck in the water all about the boat. As we got nearly opposite Ashland a ferryboat, closely packed with armed men, left the shore and headed toward us. They hailed us and signaled for us to stop. As we paid no attention to their signals, they commenced firing on us with rapidity. After they had fired two or three volleys and had wounded two of our men, the order was given for our troops to fire, which they did, and a very spirited engagement ensued, in which the mob was badly crippled. Though our cannon was on deck and finely handled by Lieutenant Bly and his men, I did not deem it necessary to fire it, as our infantry were sufficient to repulse the attack. We had five men wounded or hurt in the engagement, but none seriously. The troops acted with admirable bravery, coolness and self-possession. We will reach Lexington this morning at 9 a.m.*

John R. Allen, Major Commanding.

In his report to the adjutant general, however, Major Allen admitted the prolonged hail of fire on Ashland had been unnecessary but claimed that he had been unable to pass a cease-fire order around the *Granite State*.[173]

The man in charge of the artillery unit, Lieutenant Charles Bly, who had implored Major Allen for permission to unload his cannon toward the Ashland train,[174] said the dead and wounded in Ashland had assembled foolishly on the shore because "the people in this part of the state were prone to a morbid curiosity, and the results could not have been avoided even if veterans had a hold of the guns."[175]

In his attempt to defend the firing of the young troops on innocent citizens, the young Lieutenant Bly took the low road by laying the blame on the unarmed citizens. Bly foolishly tried to disregard the everyday importance of the Ohio River. Not only was it the major navigational route for local imports and exports, but it also served as a major entertainment venue at the time. It was common practice for folks to picnic by the river, assemble for special river events or to simply watch the river traffic. Whenever it became known that a "special" boat would be traveling on the river, large crowds would gather on the banks just to view the event. This was a common pastime, not just in Ashland, but everywhere along the river—any river. When the Swedish soprano Jenny Lind left Louisville on the riverboat *Ben Franklin* on her way to Cincinnati in April 1851, large crowds of people gathered on the riverbanks at points in between just to get a glimpse of the boat. At the conclusion of her concerts in Cincinnati, a large crowd assembled on the wharf to witness the departure of the boat that carried her.[176]

The same was true at points in between Pittsburg and the Gulf of Mexico in March 1879 when Captain Paul Boyton floated down the Ohio River in his futuristic lifesaving rubber suit. No fewer than fifteen thousand spectators assembled at the river in Cincinnati just to get a glimpse of the "Fearless Frogman" as he floated by.[177]

There was no "force" of two thousand people armed to do battle with the soldiers at Ashland. Neither was there a battery of four pieces of artillery. And if the young Major Allen really believed the *Granite* State was going to be attacked at Ashland and possibly sunk by cannon fire, why did he not order all the civilian passengers of that boat to disembark at Catlettsburg? For there were civilian passengers, including women and children aboard the *Granite State* at the time of the skirmish at Ashland. If he expected trouble at Ashland, he should have ordered all civilians off the boat at Catlettsburg. But he did not.[178]

The people gathered on the Ashland riverbank that day merely to watch the *Granite State* pass by because of its significant cargo. If there had been an armed mob assembled and expecting a clash with the soldiers, the so-called mobsters would have cleared the streets and riverbank of their women and children. The very fact of their presence on the bank and on the streets is proof positive the citizens had no idea of any trouble.[179]

Shame on Lieutenant Bly of such a lowbrow excuse for the killing of innocent citizens. "Curiosity" is simply an element of human behavior.

And that quality is not exclusive to the people of Eastern Kentucky, but to all humans everywhere. Yet Bly's publicized accusation had its desired effect. Many readers and subscribers of the newspapers abroad believed the echoed sentiment that the "mob mentality" and morbid curiosity of the Ashland people was to blame for the deaths of its own innocent citizens. The soldiers of the State Guard returned to their homes to a hero's welcome by enthusiastic crowds of citizens. A poorly trained State Guard was a crude instrument to employ in such a sensitive case as this one.[180]

And untrained, they were. Adjutant General Nuckols had admitted that "much allowance must be made for want of proper military training."[181] And he, a former Confederate colonel who fought at Chickamauga, had voiced an innate prejudice against the people of Eastern Kentucky by stating, "Eastern Kentucky was an area where lawlessness was proverbial and peaceful methods and obedience to civil authority almost unknown."[182]

Here again was an attempt to publicly and discriminately label the people of Eastern Kentucky as a lawless and violent people. Apparently General Nuckols failed to remember "Bloody Monday" where political violence rocked Louisville a few years prior to the Civil War. Contention between the Democrat and the Know-Nothing Parties escalated into an all-out war that saw twenty-two people killed on Election Day in 1855 (though some estimate there were more than one hundred fatalities). Riots broke out as buildings were burned, and people were shot as they fled the burning buildings. The city had been in the possession of an armed mob that patrolled the polls in support of the Know-Nothing Party mayoral candidate, John Barbee.[183]

General Nuckols also chose to vilify Eastern Kentucky despite the continued violence and lawlessness that characterized other parts of the state in the years following the Civil War, when violence against blacks and Union sympathizers was rampant. Groups of Regulators controlled the central Kentucky counties of Anderson, Mercer, Marion and Boyle. People of both races were lynched, beaten, threatened, burned out, and entire Black communities were driven away. Henry County, in north-central Kentucky, was a place overrun with the Ku Klux Klan. On the border of Indiana, in Gallatin County, hostilities exploded into violence, and hundreds of Black citizens were forced to flee across the Ohio River.[184]

Yet in this instance, to defend the killing of innocent bystanders by the young, untrained troops of the State Guard, Nuckols publicly declared that lawlessness prevailed in the *eastern* part of Kentucky. It is notable here to remind our readers that Eastern Kentucky had remained largely loyal to the Union during the Civil War, and not only that, but a clear trend in voting had emerged in this section that was quite different from the prewar patterns. No longer did the consistent Democrat vote prevail here. There had been few slaves in this section, and though the people were leery of abolishing slavery, the removal of that institution with the Union victory did not necessarily leave these people sympathetic to the "lost cause" as was felt by those in other parts of the state.[185]

Sacrificing the lives of young, untrained soldiers and killing all the citizens of Boyd County to protect the "dignity of the law" (in this case, two criminals convicted of the most terrible crimes) became the calling cards for a black-hearted governor and his incompetent adjutant general.

Governor Blackburn, speaking of Major Allen's report, said, "I have read it and fully indorse Major Allen's action, and will send him in command of troops to Carter County when the trials begin there."[186]

The governor also said while he was deeply sorry for the dead and wounded innocent bystanders in Ashland, he could not lay any blame on the troops, and if application be made in February, he would send twelve regiments, if necessary, to uphold the law.[187]

In response, a dispatch from A.C. Campbell, one of the three members of the Citizens Committee in Ashland, read as follows:

> *We see from the press that you volunteer to send more soldiers to whip little Boyd County. We need rather help to bury our dead and nurses for our wounded. Peace on earth, good will to men.*[188]

13
RESOLVE AND RECOVERY

A meeting of the citizens was then called to provide means to take care of the suffering ones. Committees were appointed to see who needed help and to supply their wants. Sufficient money was soon raised to pay all expenses, and no pains were spared to make all the wounded as comfortable as possible. The grief and sorrow that followed are better imagined than described. The funerals of Colonel Reppert and George Keener came off at the same time—one from the Presbyterian Church and the other from the M.E. Church—the remains of both being taken to the cemetery at the same time. The occasion was a solemn one as Colonel Reppert's aged wife and beloved daughter wailed over his dead body.[189]

The people closed their houses and went to the funerals. Business houses were closed and draped in mourning. Every day some of the wounded were expected to die. The coroner, Dr. J.W. Martin, summoned a jury, and inquests were held on the bodies of Reppert and Keener. The inquests lasted several days, and many witnesses were examined. We would like to give our readers an account in detail of the horrible affair taken from the sworn statements of some of the most influential men in our county, who were witnesses of it all. Our efficient coroner, a man in whose heart a desire for simple justice surmounts every other feeling, tried to procure all evidence in the case. We give the statements of Captain Will Kirker, who commanded the steamer *Granite State*, and who saw the so-called mob as the soldiers saw it, being with them:[190]

Captain Will Kirker:

I am master of the steamer Granite State *and was on my boat last Wednesday. We came to Catlettsburg with the expectation of taking the troops and prisoners. I was not looking for any trouble. Two companies came aboard the boat before I came downstairs. A man who intended to ship some hogs thought it would be dangerous and refused to ship. I then telegraphed to Cincinnati for instructions and received word to go ahead and take the hogs. If I had anticipated any danger, I would have discarded my passengers at Catlettsburg. But the young Major Allen had forcibly taken possession of the boat.*[191]

I expected to hear from Ashland if danger was anticipated. I held a consultation with my crew and concluded there would be no trouble. When at Norton Iron Works we whistled as if to land. The ferry whistled for hail and we paid no attention. I heard a report, then two or three more, from the direction of the ferry, followed by a volley from my steamer. Those on the ferry rushed to cover, and the soldiers fired again. I tried to get them to stop firing but they refused. I implored the soldiers not to fire on the citizens, "Do you not see you have silenced the ferryboat and all opposition? Then why do you keep on shooting women and men on the shore?"[192]

I considered the first volley all that was necessary to fire on the ferry. Firing from the steamer continued a distance of perhaps five hundred yards. I perceived no firing from the shore. One company was on the roof of the steamer, lying flat on the Kentucky side of the boat, with life floats and knapsacks for breastworks, and their guns resting on the railing. Another company was on the other side of the sky light. Those on the Kentucky side pointed their guns at the ferryboat. I do not think the others could have shot without shooting to shore. After passing the Monitor Furnace landing, the soldiers could not have fired at the ferryboat. I think they fired indiscriminately. The railing is from twenty-five to thirty feet above the water. We could see that the crowd on the shore consisted of men, women and children. I heard each of two soldiers say they had fired fourteen rounds, another six. The cannon was manned and ready to fire. I heard a cannon fired at Catlettsburg. I don't think there was any other there except that with the soldiers. There are no shallow places within a reasonable distance below Ashland. We were moving at the rate of eight miles an hour at the time. I had no authority on the boat between Catlettsburg and Portsmouth. I saw three of the soldiers take a drink at Catlettsburg. I thought there were fifteen or twenty persons on the bow of the ferryboat. I did not think the demonstrations indicated danger to the soldiers or their prisoners. I saw nobody armed on the shore.[193]

The Ashland Tragedy

Hamilton Davidson, superintendent of the Ashland and Ironton back line said,

> *Fifteen or twenty started out on the ferry. The shot that called forth the volley from the steamer was fired by a boy from the wharf boat with a pistol that would not carry to the* Granite State, *which was running near the Ohio shore. I saw a soldier come out of the pilot-house after the boat was at the lower end of town and take deliberate aim and fire at the citizens.*[194]

The following is an extract from Sheriff John J. Kouns's testimony, who had the prisoners in charge:

> *I am the Sheriff of Boyd County. I was on the* Granite State *last Wednesday when the boat passed Ashland. I would suppose the firing continued about two minutes. I saw no firing from the shore. Those near me seemed to fire at the ferryboat. I do not know how many shots were fired from the ferry or wharf-boat. Major Allen was in front of cabin. I heard no order given to fire. I was somewhat excited. I heard no order to cease firing. I went into the cabin when the firing commenced and stayed there.*[195]

J.C. Nelson, American Express manager on the *Granite State*, said:

> *I noticed that the soldiers were excited when we left Catlettsburg, but I felt perfectly easy in my own mind. I saw a man come on the prow of the ferry and fire, what I supposed to be a gun. That was the only shot that I saw fired. I wondered that the firing should continue for so long a time, inasmuch as I could hear no return shots. I think there were fifteen or twenty men on the ferryboat. I did not think there was any danger even if they did fire on us from the ferryboat. I noticed men, women and children on the shore, but I saw no arms of any kind. Regarding the bullet marks on the boat, there was one shot through the stove pipe that, from its location, could have been made from one of the soldiers. And in the pocket of the larboard chimney of the boat there was a perforation made by a bullet, but the bend of the iron was such as to show conclusively that it was made by a soldier on the boat. I did not see any shots fired from the shore, and I feel confident that there were none.*[196]

The Ashland Tragedy

Captain J.C. Whitten, town marshal, said,

> *I saw the ferry start out about the time the* Granite State *was passing. About the time she had straightened, two shots were fired from the wharf-boat. Then the firing commenced from the steamer. I could not hear any shots from the ferry. The man on the boiler deck fired at the ferry. Those lying on their faces behind the skylight on the hurricane deck fired at the people on top of the bank; shooting from that position their guns were elevated and wild in shooting. There was no hostile demonstration from on the shore.*[197]

John Means, ex-mayor of Ashland, testified,

> *I was on the Union Depot river balcony. I saw the* Granite State *from the time she came in sight. I saw the firing on the ferry and on the steamer. The ferry was at no time nearer than 100 yards of the steamer. Volley after volley was fired. After the first volley from the steamer, the ferry firing ceased; the boat became disabled and all on her disappeared and there was no firing afterward, but the firing from the* Granite State *continued from three to ten minutes after all opposition had ceased. I did not see or hear any shooting from the shore. I do not think the party on the* Granite State *was in danger from pistol shots, and there was not sufficient demonstration to warrant their action.*[198]

John Nist added,

> *I was standing on the ferry-boat at first. I left it and went to the wharf-boat. There were eighteen on the wharf-boat, boys and men. I saw but few armed; nothing that could reach the boat. Two shots were then fired from the wharf-boat. A man on the hurricane deck of the* Granite State *with shoulder straps rose and fired, then two shots from the ferry, and the disabling volley from the steamer. There was no firing from the grade.*[199]

We also give the evidence of Honorable John Calder, our present county judge, who was on the shore and saw the action as the people saw it.[200]

Judge John Calder said,

> *I was in the late war, in every position from that of private to first lieutenant. I had considerable experience as an officer and a private. I lost my leg at Chickamauga. If there was any necessity for firing, the*

commander of the boat should not have allowed more than twenty-five men to fire, and then to fire at the ferry. A general should not muster up a whole army to drive in a skirmish line guard. The commander showed bad military judgment. From the position some of the soldiers had behind the cabin skylight, shots could only have gone into town. I know this from my knowledge of steamboat building. The commander displayed bad military judgment in placing his men in the position they had according to testimony, or a desire to fire into town.[201]

The many other witnesses examined testified to the same in substance as those we have given. The following is the verdict of coroner's jury:

We, the jury, find upon view that the body lately before us is that of L.W. Reppert, of Boyd County, Kentucky. And that he was killed on the afternoon of November 1, 1882, by being shot through the left chest, near the heart, with a leaden bullet, killing him instantly. And that he was standing when killed aforesaid on the top of the Ohio riverbank, on Front street, in the city of Ashland, Boyd County, Kentucky. And then and there received the fatal shot which proceeded from the steamer Granite State from the gun of one of a party of Kentucky State Militia Troops then and there being under command of Major John R. Allen and acting as military guard to Ellis Craft and William Neal in custody of John J. Kouns, sheriff of Boyd County, who was conveying them by order of the Boyd Circuit Court to the jail of Fayette County, at Lexington. We find and do on our oaths declare that the killing of said L.W. Reppert as aforesaid was directly produced by a firing from the troops aforesaid under command as stated; and that the said fire by the troops, resulting in the death aforesaid, was not in the line of their duty, but was wanton and reckless. And we find Major John R. Allen, in command, responsible and culpable in directing and permitting the fire aforesaid.

Given under our hands this 13th day of November 1882. John Russell, Julius C. Miller, R.C. Poage, L.E. Veyssie, John I. Parrill, George Carp—jury.[202]

About the same decisions were given on the bodies of George Keener and Alexander Harris, with the exception of their positions when killed. The following is the verdict of the jury on the body of Willie Serey:

> *We, the jury, find that the dead body now before us is that of William Serey, of Ashland, Boyd County, Kentucky, who was killed and murdered on the 1st day of November, 1882, by being shot in the leg by a leaden ball, which ball was fired from a gun in the hands of some person on board the steamer* Granite State.
>
> *November 13th, 1882. J. Paul Jones, John Huffman, S. Casebolt, O.J. Chambers, C. Jones, John Parks—jury.*

And here, the curtain had been drawn upon the first few acts of this frightful drama, ending the chapter of that which has engraved itself too deeply to be forgotten upon the lives of many. For the dead a requiem soft and low from gentle, loving hearts will always flow. The hurrying moments, months and years driven by the hand of time, stay not for mortals' weal or woe. And blind justice, with even balanced scales treads with giant strides upon the unseen air, and in the dim and mystic future, far away, perhaps, somehow, somewhere, all will be right.[203]

Which is only to say the people of Ashland and Boyd County had resolved to see the end of justice. Though the actions and circumstances against them thus far would have caused many to faint and lose heart, this people remained steadfast in their struggle to see the guilty rightfully punished.

14
ELLIS CRAFT

Neal and Craft had been taken back to Lexington by the soldiers and safely housed in prison to await the February term of the Carter Circuit Court and whatever other developments might have arisen to the surface. The soldiers had received great praise and honor from their relatives and near friends for what they termed bravery in shooting down unarmed, unprotected, innocent men, women and children. Major John R. Allen was no longer a major but a colonel.

For a while, Craft and Neal were looked on by some to be great moral heroes who were willing to be sacrificed for the truth, while the citizens of Boyd County, and especially those of Ashland, were regarded by people who had only heard one side of the story as more savage than the wild man just from the woods and a bloodthirsty people, seeking innocent blood. But times and seasons had not changed the minds of the people in Northeastern Kentucky as to the guilt of Ellis Craft and William Neal of the crimes charged for which they were tried and convicted. As a natural result, everything had been done by the relatives and friends of the condemned men to show the possibility of an error in judgment on the part of the people and jurors.[204]

Three months more had passed, and the time for the trials of Neal and Craft was at hand. Before the trials of the two criminals, however, a special grand jury had been called by Judge Brown to meet at Catlettsburg, and special instructions were given this jury to hunt up all persons who had any connection with mobs or the hanging of George Ellis. The result of this diligent work was the indicting of some of Boyd County's citizens. No

The Ashland Tragedy

Ellis Craft, convicted of murdering Fannie Gibbons. *Public domain, courtesy of the Boyd County Public Library.*

attempt was made, however, to try those citizens who were indicted. But no investigation was conducted to how or why some innocent citizens of Ashland were shot down on the streets by soldiers on a passing steamboat. Neither did the grand jury investigate the so-called attack on the state troops by the "mob" in Ashland, citing insufficiency of time.[205]

Terrible stories had reached the ears of Governor Blackburn about mobs and rumors of mobs, and at the request of the Circuit Judge George N. Brown, five hundred soldiers were sent to Grayson with Neal and Craft.[206]

Once again, the soldiers were under the command of the young Colonel John R. Allen. This time, the entire State Guard had been ordered ready to be called out if necessary to go to Carter County for the trials.[207] One of the soldiers, Captain John W. Milam, commander of the McCreary Guards from Frankfort, accidentally shot himself in the leg while handling his pistol.[208]

It was apparent that the misuse of firearms was not limited to the enlisted men of Colonel Allen's army, and any training on the proper handling of firearms was woefully inadequate. Private John Hurley, the soldier who had accidentally shot himself in the leg while guarding the prisoners at Catlettsburg back in October, died from his wound several days after he had returned home to Mason County.[209] Blame for his death (gangrene) was attributed to the poor initial attention he had received from the physician in Catlettsburg.[210]

However, according to then Major Allen, in his official report to Adjutant General Nuckols, Hurley's wound was initially "dressed with skill by Dr. Duvall, our Battalion Surgeon, and assisted by Captain Price."[211] The same surgeon, Dr. Duvall, also dressed Captain Milam's leg wound.[212]

The soldiers arrived in Grayson, the county seat of Carter County, on February 7, 1883, amid terribly inclement weather. Freezing rain, partially frozen ground, floods and ankle-deep mud welcomed the soldiers as they set up camp on the outskirts of Grayson. The camp hospital saw the most action, as several of the soldiers had fallen ill, while the rumors of mob activity remained just that—rumors. Ellis Craft was the first of the two to be tried, but his trial had been delayed for several days due to the weather. Eighteen hours of heavy rain had caused the Ohio River to rise at a rate of ten inches per hour.[213] Trains had been delayed by washouts and landslides caused by the heavy rains, which had prevented the arrival of many witnesses.[214]

The bill of expenses to the state for guarding these two criminals at Grayson would rival the amount of the physicians who attended President Garfield. In addition to wages paid, the cost of feeding the troops, the officers, and thirty-four cavalry horses plus the maintenance of the camp hospital would exceed $3,000 per day.[215]

After the third delay, it was determined Neal's trial would be postponed until the next term of court, which would be held in August. It was reckoned by many, and hoped by some, the delays, plus the twenty-two-mile trek to Grayson, would cause the interest of Boyd Countians to fade. But not so! This was a people who had encountered a most horrible crime committed in their midst against their townsfolk. These people had wrongfully borne the brunt of shame as a lawless community. And they had become targets of an imbecilic governor's untrained army wielding reckless weapons. Despite the hardships, heartaches and false accusations, their will had not been broken, for they had determined to see the end of justice.

The time allotted during this term of court would be dedicated to Craft's trial. The delays gave Jailer Tyree the time needed to spruce up the Grayson Courthouse with new paint and new lamps that made the surroundings bright, clear and attractive. It might be supposed that if he'd had a red carpet, he would have rolled it out for the celebrities—Craft and Neal.[216]

After a week of delays, the weather finally permitted the court to commence with the selection of the jury. Of the twelve men who swore to have no opinions formed about the guilt or innocence of Craft, nine of them were farmers from the far reaches of Carter County. Once the jury was seated, the indictment was read and Craft stood and boldly exclaimed, "I am not guilty. Every word of it [the indictment] is a lie!"[217]

Craft was represented by Roland C. Burns, Thomas R. Brown (son of Judge Brown) and Zack Smith from Lexington, and every effort that could be made was made to save Craft from a like sentence of the Boyd County jury. Commonwealth Attorney Stephen G. Kinner and K.F. Pritchard prosecuted this case. Rumors of mobs floated as a daily occurrence that led to uneasiness among the troops. On the first night of the trial, the camp was alarmed to hear the tramp of marching feet on Main Street. The cause for alarm, however, was a half-dozen soldiers who had drifted out of camp and were found to be marching under the influence of apple brandy.[218]

Many of the same witnesses were called who had been summoned during Craft's first trial. The prosecution did, however, present a few new witnesses who testified to having heard Craft speak of his intention to carnally know Fannie Gibbons. Samuel Alley, one of the new witnesses, testified: "I've known Ellis Craft and George Ellis for a long time. One day, in the latter part of the summer, while in the brickyard I heard Ellis Craft say that he would have intercourse with Fannie Gibbons before long. He said that in the presence of a number of hands."[219]

The defense was never able to prove an alibi for Craft (or Neal for that matter) at the time the murders were committed. They tried feverishly to impeach the original confession of Ellis and called to the stand Reverend Alexander Boering. Boering testified that he had heard Ellis make the statement in the Catlettsburg jail in January 1882 that Craft was innocent. On cross-examination, however, it was brought out that Boering was "induced" to go and hear that confession by Tilman Craft, Ellis Craft's brother.[220]

Ballard Faulkner, who was imprisoned at the Boyd County jail along with Ellis, Neal and Craft after their arrests, testified again while in his presence Ellis proclaimed Craft innocent. On cross-examination, it was proved that the prisoners in the jail had threatened Ellis with violence if he would not recant his confession and declare Craft innocent.[221]

A most dramatic scene occurred during this trial when Caroline Thomas, the mother of the murdered girl, Emma Carico, was called to the witness stand. A death-like stillness settled over the courtroom as this handsome woman strode softly and slowly toward the stand. Traces of countless mournful tears had lined her grief-stricken cheeks. It was one thing to know her child's life had been unfairly and prematurely ended as if it mattered not. But it was quite another thing to sit there and look at the faces of the convicted men who found such vicious pleasure in doing so. After an extended time of complete silence, prosecuting attorney Pritchard asked, "Is Emma Carico your child?"

Through a choked and heartbroken voice, she replied, "She *was* my child." Tears trickled down her cheeks, and the attorneys on both sides bowed their heads as their eyes filled with tears. The hearts of the whole audience had been struck, as sympathy for the tearful mother could not be restrained.[222]

Final arguments were made expertly by both the defense, and the prosecution and the jury retired. The jury had been a good one and favorable to the defense, so they thought. They had expected a verdict of acquittal or, at the very least, a hung jury. Twenty minutes later, the jury returned to a filled courtroom with its verdict. "We the jury, find the defendant guilty as charged in the indictment, and fix his punishment at death." Craft showed no emotion, and the audience in the courtroom received the verdict with silent satisfaction.[223]

Ellis Craft was then asked by the court if he had anything to say as to why judgment should not be pronounced against him:

> *Well I can say one thing—I am not guilty of that charge. I did not have time to get all my witnesses that I ought to have had, and don't consider that I had a fair trial. I know that I am clear of that. I never even thought of putting hands on them children. The father and mother of those children are here, and I can tell them that I never put a hand on those children in my life. You might as well take a child just born and hang him as hang me for the crime. The closest I was to the house that night was when I was asleep. I did not see Neal or Ellis that night, and the last time I saw any of the Gibbons children was on the Wednesday before, when I saw little Fannie and spoke to her, until the next morning when I was called to the fire.*
>
> *Gentlemen, I can stand on the scaffold and take a solemn oath between me and high Heaven and swear that I am as clear of that crime as the angels in Heaven. But let me tell you, and don't you forget it that the day will come when it will stand out that I am innocent of that crime. I was better raised. I had more respect for myself, and the people with whom I was associated, and respected the children and Mrs. Gibbons. I am glad today that I stand here with a clear conscience and tell these people that I am innocent of the crime. There is not a man in the state of Kentucky can say truthfully that I am guilty. If every man in the state was as clear of that charge as I am, Mrs. Gibbons would have her children with her, and her house would be standing, and would not take the State Guard to protect the prisoners. But I hear it all with patience; but the day will come when this thing will be made clear.*[224]

Finally, Craft's monotonous rambling was interrupted when Martha Gibbons sprang to her feet and cried, "Oh, my children! My children! If only my children were here to say one word to me!" Oh, if only the graves could speak, as Abel's blood cried from the ground to the Almighty. The poor mother's anguish was felt by everyone within earshot of her voice, as she screamed, "Let me out of this place!"[225]

Judge Brown stated that the objections offered by Craft were not sufficient, the trial had been according to the rules of law and he had been ably defended. He was tried by a jury of sensible men, and it remained his painful duty to pronounce the judgment of the Court: "That you be taken to the jail of the county, and there confined until May 25 when you be taken between sunrise and sunset and hanged by the neck until dead."[226]

The evening before, considerable excitement was aroused with the arrest of Corporal Ed Moore of the Lexington Guards for drunkenness and disorderly conduct. He had run about frightening little children, and when confronted, he resisted arrest and it was not until he was bayonetted in the arm by one of the guards that he surrendered to the arresting officials.[227]

The soldiers returned the prisoners to Lexington. And Craft's case was again taken to the Court of Appeals. The soldiers were glad to be going home and relieved there had been no trouble with any so-called mob. There had been no conflict or even any appearance of one.[228]

In fact, many of the soldiers, particularly among those of the Louisville Legion, felt they had received cordial and hospitable treatment from the citizens of this section. Among the soldiers who had closely guarded the two prisoners, a feeling had emerged that William Neal had been on the verge of making a confession. The thought was if Neal had been separated from Craft for any length of time, he would have made a clean breast of the matter even if Craft had been convicted. But it had also been noted that Neal, like George Ellis, appeared to be under Craft's control and was afraid of him.[229]

There had been much discussion in camp among the Louisville Legion to withdraw from the State Guard. Major Brown of that legion said,

> *There is a general feeling that the Legion as a body has been badly treated by the adjutant general and state authorities. The boys are almost as a unit in favor of leaving the State Guard. We were organized for a Home Guard and have received more support from the city than the state, though as to whether or not we can withdraw is a question for the adjutant general to decide.*[230]

During their encampment at Grayson, the guards suffered through extremely harsh weather—ice, sleet, snow, rain, mud. And without having been supplied with proper equipment to combat the elements, several became severely ill and at least one member of the Louisville Legion died from exposure a few days after his return home.[231]

A month later, it became a fact that the unanimous opinion among those in the ranks of the Louisville Legion that it was their duty to sever their connection with the state at once and withdraw from the State Guard.[232]

It is notable to recognize the difference between the State Guard and the Home Guard. Simon Bolivar Buckner revitalized the Kentucky state militia in 1860, and it became known as the pro-Southern State Guard. Union loyalists in the state had organized their own forces called the Home Guard.[233]

While Civil War sentiments and sympathies lingered long after the conflict ended in wartorn Kentucky, they remained distinguished for a period of time by the State Guard and Home Guard.

May 25, 1883, was the date set for Craft's execution, but he was not hanged on that day. Neither was Neal tried at the August term of the Carter Circuit Court. Everything in that line appeared to stop, it was said, on account of Governor Blackburn, who had formed the habit of pardoning without any regard to the nature of the crime committed. Therefore, it was deemed advisable to wait until the old gentleman stepped down and out.[234]

During all this time, since the crimes were committed, Detective Alf Burnett, of Charleston, West Virginia, continued to work on the theory Black men had committed the crime and not Ellis, Neal and Craft. On occasions when it was thought it would have the most effect on the courts to the advantage of Neal and Craft, Burnett would spring his theory. He gained enough ground in his efforts that Detective John T. Norris had resurfaced and joined him in his pursuit. Burnett had set his sights on a Black man, William Direly, and was self-assured an arrest was forthcoming.[235]

At last it came to a climax. Burnett had employed a Black man by the name of Cabell to help work up the case, and about June 10, 1883, they found Direly, a former citizen of Ashland, in Columbus, Ohio, and brought him to Catlettsburg and cast him into prison under the charge of the murder of the Gibbons children and Emma Carico. The *Cincinnati Enquirer* spread the news abroad that the right parties had been found and one of them had been arrested and had confessed to the crime and the proof was positive. This news spread far and near and was believed by thousands who heard and read the account. But the whole affair was fraudulent. Seeing the folly of Burnett's theory and to save himself from any further embarrassment, Detective Norris retired from the case with the opinion that Burnett's charges were without foundation.[236]

Norris sent the following dispatch to the Citizens Committee in Ashland:

> *I have no connection whatever in the proposed detection of the negroes for the murder of the Gibbons family. I was called in the case yesterday, twenty-four hours after Direly was arrested. I accompanied Burnett with the prisoner as far as Gallipolis for the purpose of consultation only, and then returned to Columbus in order to ascertain what truthfulness there was in the statements made, and, after an impartial investigation, I have found the facts to be so much in variance with the statements made to me, and against the truth that I must decline to act with him in the matter. It looks to me like a big scheme manufactured for some private purpose, and that of very poor material at that.*[237]

Direly was tried, and after all the produced testimony was heard, the case was submitted without argument and the prisoner was discharged. Alf Burnett said the court had done right, and he gave up on the case, admitting it was a mistake.[238]

It was said Burnett had been inspired to work up the theory by his spite against Marshal Heflin, who had taken the work of detection out of his hands a year and half ago.[239]

As the court had adjourned, some of Direly's friends were involved in a ruckus, and Cabell was wounded in the leg by a pistol shot. Bystanders, including Tilman Craft, said he accidentally shot himself while attempting to draw his pistol.[240] Many of Direly's friends and those in the Black community felt they had known all along there would be a great effort made to have the Ashland murders "laid on a nigger."[241]

The vindication of Direly was thorough and complete. In fact, the whole farcical case took a turn in the opposite direction, as Detective Burnett found himself arrested and charged with kidnaping Direly.[242]

Soon after the sham trial of Direly, the Court of Appeals ruled on the Craft case. In a rather lengthy opinion offered by Justice Hines, the court affirmed the judgment of the lower court. Craft's attorneys were given thirty days to file a petition for a rehearing but decided against it, whereby Craft said he would die like a man and hoped to meet his friends in Heaven.[243]

The only hope that Craft's friends now had was to influence the new governor, J. Proctor Knott, which they tried to do in various ways—not for a pardon, but only for a respite until after the trial of Neal, at which time they hoped to introduce new testimony in the case that would clear both Neal and Craft of the crime. It was the same tale by which they had previously fooled Governor Blackburn—the discovery of new evidence—yet at his second trial, they failed to produce any such evidence. Governor Knott patiently examined the records of both trials that convicted Craft but could find nothing that would justify him to further interfere with the operation of the law.[244]

He then set October 12 for Craft to hang at Grayson and so ordered. A petition was gotten up and a few signatures were procured and the same was forwarded to Governor Knott, still he refused to grant the respite.[245]

The Sheriff of Carter County had applied to the governor for soldiers to guard Craft, but Knott informed the sheriff that he could provide his own guard. Apparently, Governor Knott was more frugal than his predecessor, who had spent more than $60,000 of taxpayer money to "protect" the two convicted criminals.[246]

In his reply to the Carter County sheriff, Governor Knott wrote, "The people everywhere should realize that they must rely upon the law, and not upon military force for protection." If the governor's predecessor (Luke Blackburn) had taken a similar stance, it is likely the massacre on the river would have been avoided and many innocent lives spared.[247]

After it became clear that all attempts at saving Craft had been exhausted, people who knew and had been afraid of him began to speak out. His father was a good Christian man and a minister of the Baptist Church, and his mother was a woman of more than ordinary intelligence, charitable and noble in many respects. But Craft, at an early age, began a career of criminality that for devilry and pure cussedness has doubtless no parallel in history and ended in him being placed behind bars, only to be freed when the law, by just decree, sees his body dangling in the air until he is dead.[248]

From his earliest boyhood, he was overbearing and always in trouble or getting someone else in trouble. He began his criminal career by seducing a very pretty young girl and, under promise of marriage, persuaded three other innocent girls to yield to his devilish passions. As a result of his illicit behavior, he fathered three children. One of his victims left home soon after Craft accomplished his ruin and went to Portsmouth, Ohio, where she took up in a house of ill repute.[249]

He had been arrested twice by the Ashland city marshal and several times in Catlettsburg for disorderly conduct. He had no respect for anyone and saw all women as lewd persons, subject to the exercise of man's passions. Many wives, daughters and children were afraid of Craft, and respectable society shunned him. His character had always been bad, and he was viewed as a coward and one who would take advantage of a person at every opportunity. He would brag beforehand about what he intended to do. People here were afraid to make lawful complaints against him for fear their property would be burned or their lives sacrificed. At the time of his second indictment for the murders of Robbie and Fannie Gibbons, Craft had three other indictments against him for other crimes he had allegedly committed.[250]

On that previously mentioned occasion when he shot his pistol at the businessman, Proctor, for coming to the defense of his wife, Craft was arrested. He protested his innocence with his usual jargon, declaring he was as innocent of that crime as a newborn babe and called on the angels of Heaven to witness his assertions of innocence.[251]

When Proctor and his wife failed to testify against Craft before the grand jury for fear of their lives, the case against him was dismissed. In short, Craft had committed many crimes and was considered a very dangerous man to have in any community.[252]

Once the original confession of George Ellis became public, reporters flocked to Ashland with intentions of interviewing him and hearing his story straight from the horse's mouth. Many of them were left with the feeling Ellis was holding something back and had more to tell. Some thought there may have been a fourth man involved in the crime whom Ellis refused to name. Others thought Ellis may have had a greater part in the crime than he claimed. One reporter from the *Cincinnati Enquirer* thought he had uncovered the reason for Ellis's perceived reluctance to tell everything:

> *There is a part of George Ellis's confession that has never been published, which makes out the crime perpetrated in that little cottage on that frightful Friday night even more horrid, repulsive and sickening than the most hardened villain ever could conceive were it left to the imagination alone. It was this: The struggles of the girls were terrific, and both of them came near escaping Neal and Craft. It was, as has been stated before, Craft who violated Fannie Gibbons. He choked her violently in attempting to overcome her, and remarked, "I fix you so you can't kick," George Ellis says that while Craft was in the act of sexual commerce with Fannie Gibbons, he* [Ellis] *placed his hand on the young girl's shoulder and she never moved, but was evidently dead, so that the detestable brute, Craft, violated the poor girl in death. Her head was afterward mashed in to make sure of the hellish work.*[253]

On the morning of October 9, Sheriff Holcomb and his posse of nine men went to Lexington and returned the next day to Grayson with Craft. The Reverend J.P. Pinkerton, Craft's spiritual adviser, then had a long conversation with him in the jail and the following morning took him in a buggy to the Little Sandy River, one-half mile distant from town, to baptize him. It was a queer sight to see a man marched to the river to be baptized while being guarded by twenty-five men with guns. Four hundred people witnessed the scene, and though most believed Craft to be guilty, a collective feeling of sorrow for the doomed man enveloped the silent crowd.[254]

That same evening, Craft received several letters, which encouraged the hope that something would interfere in time to save him. One of these letters was from Detective Alf Burnett, in which he informed Craft that he had written a letter to Governor Knott protesting his (Craft's) innocence and declaring Direly the guilty one (even though Burnett had given up on that theory months before). He also received a letter from his brother, Tilman Craft, who had worked so steadily from the beginning to try to prove his brother's innocence. From the letter it is clear even Tilman was not convinced of his brother's innocence:

> *Dear brother Ellis: This may be the last letter you will ever receive from me. I have fought the fight through for you. I have only quit the field when the last resource has been exhausted. I want you to tell the truth tomorrow. What you say on that day must not be disputed before me. Tell the truth! In Heaven I hope we will meet. If they have done you wrong in this world, in the upper court, beyond the grave, we'll know all. If they persecuted you wrongfully, woe unto them in the everlasting life, if you are innocent. You may be cast down here, but in eternity James Heflin, A.C. Campbell, John Russell, and D.D. Geiger cannot harm you, for then all will be well. My brother tell the truth and then I will be satisfied. Every line I have written causes me to drop a tear. Dear brother, in the years to come, when the work is finished, stand on the shore of the "dark river" and hold a light, my brother, so that I may pass over. If you are only innocent, and die as such, "Praise God!" the warfare is ended, the victory won, and I will say, "peace on earth, good will to men." God says, "Vengeance is mine, I will repay the wicked." But oh! That dear heart-broken mother that lies at the feet of the Master today. Only He that knows all hearts knows her sorrow. There are those that pass through all the hardships of this world, but in Heaven they are rich—rich unto everlasting life. I praise God that there is justice in the other world. Die with the truth upon your lips and the praise of Him who has said, "Come unto me all ye that are heavy laden, and I will give you rest." My dear brother, I know you need rest. What you have suffered is only known to Him who says, "Tis enough, come up higher." Praise God, and die telling the truth, is all I ask.*
> *Your brother, T. Craft*[255]

At 12:34 p.m. on October 12, Craft was taken from the jail and conducted to the street. There a buggy waited to take him the gallows. Armed guards surrounded the buggy as it passed by houses filled with curious spectators. He had donned his new black suit, which sported a turn-down collar, and black necktie. Pinned on his breast were a few tuberoses sent to him by some kind woman. He also held a large bouquet of flowers sent to him by an admiring female.[256]

A crowd of about five thousand men, women and children congregated to witness the first hanging in Carter County and the most famous hanging that Eastern Kentucky had ever known.[257]

As the noose dangled behind him, Craft spoke the words given in the first chapter that bear not repeating here. He declared over and over his innocence and exhorted the people how to live, how to teach their children and to take warning from him. After he was through speaking, he sang a hymn and then made a tearful prayer. He was followed by Reverend Pinkerton in a prayer. As Pinkerton prayed, Craft occasionally made tearful interjections. When he arose, however, his eyes were dry and his face as calm as ever.[258]

The handcuffs were then changed, and his hands put behind him and a rope wound around his legs. The black cap was then drawn over his face and the rope placed around his neck. He then declared he was innocent, the trap door was knocked from under him and he was launched into eternity. The trap was sprung at 1:15 p.m., and the body was cut down at 1:30 p.m.

Thus ended the life of Ellis Craft.

Craft's body was taken by his brother for burial at a graveyard on the farm of John M. Burns. It is a small graveyard containing no tombstones with small unmarked sandstones among weeds on a lonely hill.[259]

15

WILLIAM NEAL

Now that the ringleader of one of the worst crimes ever committed against humanity was gone, William Neal, the seemingly forgotten man in some respects, was again brought to Grayson in April 1884 and given another trial. It was basically a rehash of his first trial, with the same result. During the trial, Martha Gibbons was called to the witness stand amid profound silence. She was asked if she ever saw her children after she had returned to Ashland. At this, she broke down, tears flooded her face and she could speak no more. Jury members began to weep, and counsel spoke no further word.[260]

As court adjourned, Martha voiced the hope that this would be the last trial that would call on her as a witness. "It is killing me," she somberly said.[261]

Judge Rice then set July 18 for the execution. Here, we remind our readers that according to George Ellis's original confession it was he, William Neal, who proposed to kill the girls, Fannie Gibbons and Emma Carico. The case was again taken to the Court of Appeals and again the decision of the lower court sustained. By the time of the Court of Appeals ruling, the day set for execution had passed, and Governor Knott fixed February 27, 1885, for the execution.[262]

Over three years had now passed since the crime was committed, and no new developments had been made. As a last resort, Neal's wife, accompanied by a minister and several others from Mount Sterling, took a petition to the governor to have the sentence changed from death to life imprisonment. Governor Knott being absent, Lieutenant Governor Hindman acted and,

William Neal, convicted of murdering Emma Carico. *Public domain, courtesy of the Boyd County Public Library.*

after hearing their case, said he would consider the matter, but he later telegraphed to Neal's friends that he would have nothing to do with the case and the law must take its course.[263]

Neal was again taken to Grayson, and all preparations were made for the execution on the day set. The people gathered from every direction to see the last act of the horrible tragedy. Extra cars were put on the railroads—all crowded with people—and by ten o'clock, the town of Grayson was crowded with disappointed people. The night before, Lieutenant Governor Hindman's sympathy got the better of his judgment and he sent a telegram to Sheriff Holcomb to have the prisoner removed to Mount Sterling at once. This was done by taking Neal on foot, during the night, to Leon Station. He was then put on a train to Mount Sterling. The people who had gathered were aggravated, to say the least of it. The end of justice was again thwarted, and through the medium of gossip, word was quickly spread that Neal had been pardoned by the governor. But Hindman had not granted a pardon, merely a respite until March 27. And the people returned to their homes to await another month.[264]

The news of the respite gave Neal a breath of renewed hope. While confined at Mount Sterling, he continued to proclaim his innocence with a brash self-assurance. To the newspaper men who gathered to hear statements from him, Neal said, "I am innocent and never felt that I would be hung." He made the claim that George Ellis was drunk and had been bulldozed into making his original confession by rich men.[265]

The people of Mount Sterling who believed in his innocence felt they should do what they could in his behalf. One Patrick Punch, an ex-marshal of that town who also had an abiding faith in Neal's innocence, went at the request of the citizens and of his own will to hunt up some evidence by which at least suspicion might be thrown onto some other parties and create reasonable doubt about Neal's guilt. After traveling through the upper counties of Kentucky and a portion of West Virginia and hunting up everything that could be found connected with the case, Punch concluded Neal was the right man and the gallows was the right place for him. Neal himself, however, had some hope and wrote a letter to Lieutenant Governor Hindman, who had shown him so much mercy before. In his letter, Neal pleaded innocence and begged that his sentence should be changed to life imprisonment. The lieutenant governor had received more light on the case or had hardened his heart and replied, "I am constrained to say I cannot comply with your request."[266]

On Thursday, March 26, 1885, Neal was brought to Grayson. The coffin that had been prepared a month before and the gallows on which Craft was executed awaited him. On Friday morning the people again gathered, but not near so many as on former occasions. Religious services were held in the jail. Neal joined in the exercise and said he had been converted seven years ago and had made perfect reconciliation with his Master and was going to Heaven. In reply to a friend he said, "I can't confess because I ain't guilty. I've got to look out for myself and you needn't urge me. I won't do it."[267]

Neal was taken from the jail at 12:45 p.m. When he arrived at the gallows, he ran up the steps, glanced at the rope and said in a clear voice, "This is no place to tell a lie. I am not guilty of the heinous crime of which I stand convicted. Someday my innocence will be established." The program had been arranged for a half-hour speech from Neal, then reading from the Bible and singing, but this was cut short by Neal turning to the audience and saying, "I bid you one and all farewell." The black cap and noose were adjusted and the trap sprung, and the last one of the trio dropped into eternity.[268]

Sufficient money was donated by a few of the citizens of Ashland to pay the expenses of taking the body to Catlettsburg, where it was given to his friends for interment at his father-in-law's farm at a spot designated by Neal shortly before his execution.[269]

The Honorable Daniel K. Weis, the attorney who had represented George Ellis at his trial for murder, later made public a conversation he'd had with Ellis prior to his trial:

Before Neal or Craft had been tried, we had frequent consultations with Ellis, and we were particular to impress it upon his mind that by his confession he had virtually fastened the rope around his own neck and sealed his own doom. And we warned him of his awful situation and told him not to add another horror to his crime by accusing Neal and Craft of a most horrible crime if they were innocent. In these interviews with the warning before him, he [Ellis] always said that Neal and Craft were guilty as he had charged them. Afterwards, in the presence of Major Brazee, whose friendship for his family in West Virginia induced him to come to Boyd County as a volunteer counsel; Ellis was warned by Major Brazee and myself of the terrible crime he would commit if he swore away the lives of Neal and Craft, he again reaffirmed as true what he had stated before, that Neal and Craft were equally or more guilty than himself.[270]

Three years, three months and three days intervened between the time of the crime and the final punishment.

16
COMMENTARY

The Ashland Tragedy left an enduring sentiment in the hearts and minds of the people of Ashland and Boyd County. The unforeseen pandemonium on the Ohio River that took place on that fated November 1882 afternoon seemed to have overshadowed the concern for the initial victims of the tragedy: Robbie and Fannie Gibbons and Emma Carico. And that ought not to be so. For it was their young lives that were targeted and ended by the hellish creatures who had determined to fulfill their own sinful desires. And it was the murders of those three innocent children that set in motion the ensuing chaos where agitation, excitement, vindication and retaliation led to a climate of animosity and resentment. Neighbor against neighbor, newspaper against newspaper—ultimately, the entire state had vilified a small section of its own people.

Sympathy

Though there were many victims of this horrid affair and many of their descendants are yet among us, due sympathies must first be given to the Gibbons and Thomas families. Caroline Thomas, who witnessed the fire that burned her daughter's already dead body practically beyond recognition must surely have our sympathy. One can only imagine her helpless and frantic behavior at the burning house knowing her daughter was inside the flames.

John Gibbons, who, by all accounts may not have been a saintly soul, was thrust into a national spotlight by the false accusation that he had murdered his own children. It is difficult, if not impossible, to imagine the feeling of knowing his two children had been brutally murdered and set on fire and then having also been accused of the crime. It is certainly understandable his feeling for wanting to shoot the men who were convicted of the crime.

And poor Martha Gibbons, who had lost her baby, five-year-old Harry, just months before the tragedy that saw Robbie and Fannie so brutally murdered and maimed, has our due sympathies. She must have also carried a great measure of guilt regarding the death of Emma Carico, for if she had not asked permission for her to stay the night with Fannie, she would not have been murdered that night. And not only that, but Martha also lost her son-in-law James McDonald, the father of two of her grandchildren, when he was gunned down by the State Guard at the massacre on the Ohio River, leaving the eldest Gibbons daughter, Florence, a widow for the remainder of her life. The Gibbons family has our deepest sympathies. Despite all the heartache that Martha endured, a little ray of sunshine interrupted her tragic life when her grandson was crowned handsomest baby of the Ashland Fair in 1883. Out of fifteen competitors, the son of Anna (Gibbons) Nist and John Nist won the premium prize of what was said to have been the most attractive feature of the fair.[271]

And of course, sympathies are given for the families of the innocent victims who were gunned down by Major Allen's undisciplined and untrained militia who had indiscriminately fired their weapons on the crowd of spectators gathered on the riverbank and streets on that fateful November day. And there must be sympathies given to the families of the soldiers who died while protecting the prisoners. At least one died from a self-inflicted gunshot, and others (number unknown) died as a result of suffering from the wintry elements in Grayson while camped there.

We also extend our sympathies to the families of George Ellis, William Neal and Ellis Craft. The families are not to blame for the actions and fates that befell the trio convicted of the horrendous crimes. Those families also suffered heartache and heartbreak untold during and after this renowned ordeal.

Many people suffered and lives were transformed—none for the better. In addition to the heartache and heartbreak, good men were slandered, honest men were challenged and the press reigned supreme.

Questions

Nearly 140 years have passed since that terrible Christmas Eve, yet after all the facts have been examined, a few questions remain. Why was George Ellis forced to go the Gibbons house that night? Apparently, his work at the brickyard left something to be desired, and on at least one occasion, Craft and Neal covered for him so he would not have lost pay or have gotten fired. According to Craft, this made Ellis mad enough to want them dead.[272]

However, considering Craft's overbearing personality, it is more reasonable to think they held this over Ellis's head in the form of a favor owed them. Also, Craft and Neal had taken Ellis in their confidence regarding their intentions that fateful night and believed it best to have Ellis join them, thinking he would be less likely to tell what he knew if he were an active participant in the deed. And there was the suspicion that the three of them had become fast friends who engaged, as gang members, in local robberies, thefts and petty crimes.[273]

Was George Ellis insane? The facts are clear that both Craft and Neal professed innocence throughout the whole drama, all the way up until each dropped from the gallows. Craft, Neal and Alf Burnett had made statements to the effect that Ellis was insane. However, from sworn testimony, George Ellis had never shown any signs of insanity prior to the murders. He was described as a good, quiet citizen of good character and a very industrious young man who always seemed to conduct himself in a proper manner. Three times Ellis allegedly recanted on his original confession. The first time was when he was unwisely jailed alongside Craft and Neal at Catlettsburg. There, and by sworn testimony, he recanted due to the threat of bodily harm. Neither of the other two alleged confessions came from the lips of George Ellis. And each time he quashed those reports when given the opportunity to verify, or nullify, them. Regarding his alleged retraction told by the jailbird, John Adkins, Ellis said, "It is an infamous lie. I have told the truth from the first and I will stick to it till I die." He reiterated his original confession while aboard the *Mountain Boy* during the river chase and to his tearful wife during a somber visitation. He did the same in private conversation with his attorney, D.K. Weis, and once again on his hanging tree. There was never an attempt by any of the defense attorneys for Neal and Craft to prove insanity on the part of George Ellis.

How did Ellis's last words on the hanging tree become known? Many times, a masked member of a lynch mob would later speak out without fear of retribution. Also, as quietly and covertly a masked mob attempted to operate, it would oftentimes attract an audience. Any member of the crowd or mob could have reported the last words of George Ellis.

Perhaps the biggest question that begs an answer is why wasn't George Ellis protected by the soldiery like Neal and Craft? There is something noticeably suspicious about this. If Judge Brown and Governor Blackburn were honestly intent on protecting the dignity of the law, why then was Ellis simply hung out to dry? The governor had gone to great lengths to protect the lives of Neal and Craft. But why not Ellis? Was it because he was a rat, a tattletale, a stool pigeon? Or perhaps his life sentence would have added to the already overcrowded prison system, which "Lenient Luke" had worked so hard to reform. Knowing the agitation and feelings that pervaded the people of Ashland, along with the newspapers' continuous goading for a lynching, it would seem that a trap had been set with Ellis as the bait. The trap was sprung with his lynching, which resulted in the branding of Ashland as a lawless, mob-rule town. And with this, Ashland and Boyd County were virtually excommunicated from the state as the ex–war criminal governor effectively declared war by threatening to kill every man, woman and child in Boyd County. It is not a pretty thought, but one that unavoidably must be given a measure of consideration since the end result lessened the strain on the prison system (by one) and sparked (lynching) Governor Blackburn's declaration of war on Boyd County.

Who was responsible for lynching George Ellis? That question may never be answered. It is true most of the jurors were inclined to fasten the death penalty on Ellis but were persuaded by a lone juror to settle for life imprisonment. Whether the lynch mob was an organized group of Regulators, a frustrated band of local citizens or friends of Neal and Craft, clearly it would seem to have been Neal and Craft to reap the most benefit from Ellis's death.

The State Guard

It is a mistake to think of the Kentucky militia at that time in view of today's disciplined and well-trained army. Though not all, many of the young volunteers at the time were pooled from the dregs of society, some having never shot or even held a weapon. Adjutant General Nuckols admitted the State Guard lacked proper military training. And the man chosen to command those troops, Major John Allen, was said to have been "wholly unfit for his assigned duties." That became obvious when he failed to order the civilians to disembark the *Granite State* at Catlettsburg, believing his troops would face a two-thousand-member armed mob at Ashland with four pieces of artillery. He also failed to "hold his men well in hand" as ordered, evidenced by his inability to pass a cease-fire order around the *Granite State*.

Major Allen also overstepped his authority, as he was ordered to be "subordinate to the Sheriff of Boyd County." According to the testimony of Captain Kirker, Allen commandeered the steamer *Granite State*. He then gave the order to fire sans consultation with Sheriff Kouns. From his own testimony, Sheriff Kouns did not give the order to fire—neither did he hear an order given to fire. In his official report to Adjutant General Nuckols, Major Allen stated that Sheriff Kouns had relinquished authority to him. Yet in his official report to the governor, Allen shrewdly stated, "*The* order was given to fire." He refrained from saying, "*I* gave the order to fire," presenting the implication that he was, in fact, acting as a subordinate to the sheriff, as ordered.[274]

Again, blame should not be placed on the soldiers for firing on the ferryboat. By all accounts, the ferryboat posed a threat (albeit a minimal one) to the soldiers, many of whom were no doubt anxious and scared (and inexperienced, according to Major Allen). And the first shot that triggered the melee did not come from the soldiers. Yet the threat quickly expired with the disabling of the ferryboat. At that time, the cease-fire order should have been given and observed. Nine years after the fact, a man named Robert Lother, who was wounded in the abdomen during the Ohio River massacre, claimed that it was he who fired the first shot that provoked the initial volley from the *Granite State*.[275]

Neal and Craft

Interestingly, the convictions of both Neal and Craft were won largely based on the testimonies of the two women who corroborated George Ellis's Christmas Day cemetery meeting. Certainly, Ellis's whole testimony was damaging. And his telling of the positions of the bodies, the oilcan, the ax, the crowbar and so on—all verified by the responders to the fire—was difficult for the defense teams to successfully counter. But the cemetery meeting was the most damaging part of his testimony that could have been, and was, verified by other witnesses.

Though neither Craft nor Neal had been able to establish a satisfactory alibi, they managed to gain a small measure of support locally by friends and family and a larger measure of support from those afar who believed in their innocence. And there are those today who believe in their innocence. But as Patrick Punch, the ex-marshal of Mount Sterling who initially believed in the innocence of William Neal, discovered, after conducting his own investigation, Neal was the right man convicted and the gallows was the right place for him. William Neal brought suspicion on himself early on by voicing his concern that he might be suspected of the crime and that he might no longer be safe living in Geiger's Addition. Elder M. Harkins was also disposed to believe in Neal's innocence when he accompanied the sheriff during the reading of the death warrant at Grayson. However, after talking to Neal in his cell about death and dying, he came away with all doubt removed about Neal's guilt believing justice would be thwarted if he were to be saved from the gallows.[276]

Craft's life story speaks volumes for itself, and though Detective Alf Burnett worked tirelessly to prove Craft's innocence, Burnett was among the first to suspect Ellis Craft of the terrible crime. At the funeral of the girls, Craft drove a carriage that carried one of the bodies to the graveyard. He also helped the undertaker lay out the bodies. While doing so, the undertaker noticed that Craft trembled like a leaf, so much so that he could hardly perform the task. The undertaker said to himself at the time that he believed Craft might have had something to do with the murders. In conversation with Jailer Tyree at Grayson just hours before his execution, Craft said, "If I was guilty, I would not own it."[277]

Conclusion

As noted in the beginning chapter, the people of Ashland were largely a hardworking, God-fearing, enterprising people who wished only the best for the community. The awful crime committed at the Gibbons house on that Christmas Eve triggered a three-year period that saw their mettle sorely tested. Their collective indignation at the vicious murders effectively and unjustly put them on the defensive. They became targets of verbal jabs at their ability to conduct justice by law until that right was snatched from them. Soon afterward they became the physical targets of an untrained army wielding careless weapons that sapped the life right out of them. Meanwhile, the convicted perpetrators of the heinous crime were heralded as heroes and viewed by those afar as victims of a lawless and barbarous community. We live, at times, in an upside-down world.

From the time Judge Brown made his initial request to the governor for the State Guard to protect the prisoners until the last man dropped from the gallows, an undercurrent silently flowed throughout the drama that emanated lingering Civil War sentiments. A former Confederate war-criminal governor, along with the former Confederate colonel adjutant general, plus a circuit judge with Southern sympathies, commanded the political machine that ran roughshod over the Boyd County citizens. The citizens of Ashland were dismayed and terribly wronged by Judge Brown's refusal to accept their pledge of protecting the prisoners. For if he had, perhaps the hasty designation of a mob rule community could have been quickly erased, perhaps the lynching of George Ellis might have been prevented and perhaps the river massacre may never have happened.

But the people of Ashland and Boyd County persevered and eventually gained a measure of vindication when justice finally righted the wrong. A time of sorrow, grief and bitterness naturally followed, and some forgave while others tried to forget this mournful period of Ashland's past, a most infamous part of Kentucky's history.

End

BRIEF BIOGRAPHIES

JOHN MEANS was the mayor of Ashland at the time of the Ashland Tragedy murders in December 1881. He served in that office from October 1881 to June 1882. He was born on September 21, 1829. He was a leader in the banking and iron industries. He served as the vice president of the Ashland National Bank and led the growing iron business of the Means family—one of the companies that created massive enterprises out of the disorganized and weakened industry that emerged from the Civil War. His father, Thomas Means, built the Buena Vista furnace. John Means was a patron of education and donated the land in Ashland where the school for African American children was located. He witnessed the massacre on the river by the Kentucky Militia and testified to such. At his death in February 1910, his estate was appraised at nearly $700,000

W.C. IRELAND was born in Mason County, Kentucky, on November 28, 1823. He received a good education, chiefly at the private schools of Mason and Lewis Counties. In 1845, he went to Clarksburg, Lewis County, where he studied law and was admitted to the bar in 1848. In 1852, he removed to Greenup County, where he established a large practice and became one of the leading men at the bar of Eastern Kentucky. In 1859, he was elected to represent Greenup County in the lower house of the legislature and was reelected in 1861. He took the position against secession from the Union and was bitterly opposed to the establishment of the Southern Confederacy, yet his sympathies were very warm for the Southern people.

Brief Biographies

In 1874, he was elected circuit judge of the Sixteenth Judicial District, his term expiring in 1880. He was one of the ablest lawyers and most valuable citizens in his part of the state.

Judge George N. Brown, lawyer, statesman and jurist was born September 22, 1822, on the banks of the Ohio River in Cabell County, West Virginia, on the site of the present city of Huntington. George Newman Brown was twice married and had twelve children, five by the first marriage and seven by the second. After returning from college in 1840, he began the study of law in the office of Judge James M. Rice of Louisa and was admitted to the bar in October 1844. He practiced law in Pike and adjacent counties for sixteen years and removed to Catlettsburg in 1860 and entered into partnership with Judge Rice. During the Civil War, he was a noncombatant, but his sympathies were with the Southern people. In 1880, he was elected by the people judge of the Circuit Court. As judge on the bench, Brown was courteous, patient and impartial to hear both sides and counsel fully, then firm and fearless to decide and enforce the mandates of the law. On the bench, he won the reputation of being one of the ablest and purest jurists of Kentucky. Judge Brown died on March 10, 1901, in Catlettsburg at the age of seventy-eight.

Thomas R. Brown was the son of Judge George N. Brown and represented William Neal in his first trial and then both Neal and Ellis Craft at their second trials. Thomas Richard Brown was born on June 2, 1854, in Pikeville, Kentucky, and educated in Catlettsburg and at Danville Collegiate Institute. In 1872, he entered the University of Virginia and afterward attended the Louisville Law School. After graduating in 1876, he began the practice of law in Catlettsburg in partnership with his father, George N. Brown. He soon took high rank in his profession. He was appointed commissioner of public schools. He was elected president of the Big Sandy National Bank and was one of its charter members. Thomas R. Brown died in Catlettsburg on June 20, 1909, at the age of fifty-five.

Stephen G. Kinner was born in Lawrence County, Kentucky, on July 20, 1848. He was educated in the common schools of Boyd County at South Bend, Indiana, Center College of Danville and Ohio Wesleyan University in Delaware, Ohio. In 1868, he entered the law office of Ireland & Hampton in Catlettsburg, Kentucky. In 1874, he was elected county attorney and in 1880 elected commonwealth attorney of the Sixteenth Judicial District. In

1892, he was elected circuit judge of the district for a term of five years. He was known as a fine lawyer, an able jurist and a highly honored and respectable citizen.

ABRAM CROYSDALE (A.C.) CAMPBELL was born on November 30, 1844, and was one of the men appointed to the three-man Citizens Committee. He came from a family respected for their moral worth, who, by honest labor, strict attention to business and financial ability became wealthy. Not only did he follow in their pathway, but he also advanced on what they had so well begun. In his boyhood, he was qualified as a bookkeeper to enter the counting house of a large manufacturing establishment and was, about the close of the Civil War, elected by the directors of the Bank of Ashland as its teller. In 1868, Campbell succeeded John N. Richardson as cashier, doing business under a charter from the State of Kentucky that was organized under the laws of the United States. He continued his official position with the bank as its cashier until 1882, when he then accepted the same office at the Catlettsburg National Bank until 1887. He owned large real estate interests in Ashland and elsewhere and was one of Boyd County's solid men. A.C. Campbell died in January 1913 at the age of sixty-eight.

JOHN CALDER was born on October 26, 1834, and was one of the men appointed to the three-man Citizens Committee. John Calder fought for the Union during the American Civil War and lost a leg in the Battle of Chickamauga in 1863. Calder became a hardware merchant in Ashland and was elected county judge of Boyd County in 1882. John Calder died in July 1887 at the age of fifty-two.

JOHN RUSSELL was born near Londonderry, Ireland, on December 25, 1821, and was one of the men appointed to the three-man Citizens Committee. He was brought to this country in 1830 by his farmer father, who settled in Tyler County, now West Virginia. At the age of sixteen, he clerked in a hardware store. In 1850, he came to Kentucky and for two years was bookkeeper for the Amanda Furnace in Greenup County at $400 per year and board. He was given one-quarter interest in the profits of the whole business, and his salary increased to $1,000 per annum. He next bought an eighth interest in the Belle Fonte Furnace in 1855, forming a partnership with the owners, Thomas and Hugh Means. Russell was one of the incorporators of the Norton Iron Works, the largest in the county, with a capital stock of $800,000. He became president of the Norton Iron Works in 1877. He was also president of the Catlettsburg National Bank, president of the Means & Russell Iron company and president of the St. Clair Coke Works in Fayette County, West Virginia. He was instrumental in establishing the town of Riverview, in Greenup County, which was later (in 1873) renamed Russell in his honor. John Russell died on December 24, 1896, one day shy of the age of seventy-five.

DANIEL K. WEIS, the lawyer who represented George Ellis at his trial, was born on March 17, 1816, in Pennsylvania. During his life, he had held very responsible positions, including postmaster of Ashland and editor of the *Ashland Express*. He was known to have been better acquainted with the political issues of the day than almost any man in his part of the state. D.K. Weis died on April 15, 1910, in Ashland at the age of ninety-four.

ALPHEUS W. BURNETT was born on July 9, 1850, in New Bedford, Pennsylvania. He was educated at Grove City College in Mercer County, Pennsylvania. After teaching school for two years, he moved to Wayne County, West Virginia, and published a newspaper, the *Advocate*. He then moved to Huntington and became editor of the *Advertiser*. In 1876, he moved to Charleston, West Virginia, and continued to work in the newspaper business. In 1878, he organized the Eureka Detective Agency, which was incorporated on April 21, 1880. Possibly his most heralded exploit included being among a group of detectives involved in the capture of Dave Stratton, one of the participants in the Hatfield/McCoy feud. Alf Burnett died on November 1, 1892, at the age of forty-two.

JAMES ALTIG HEFLIN was born on July 4, 1845, and spent his boyhood in Maysville, Kentucky. In February 1864, at the age of eighteen, he enlisted as a private in Company H, Eleventh Kentucky Cavalry. On March 12 of the same year, he was promoted to sergeant. He was a participant in many warm engagements with the enemy and was conspicuous for his bravery, one of his most prominent virtues. In 1872, he was elected city marshal of Maysville. He was commissioned a deputy U.S. marshal under U.S. Marshal Crittenden and again under the succeeding U.S. marshal, Andrew Auxier. For sixteen years, he had practical control of police affairs in Maysville and was never known to have wavered in his duty. While it was as a public officer that he was best and most favorably known, he was nonetheless appreciated as a private citizen and as a friend. Generous and kind-hearted and of a warm, impulsive nature, he was ever ready to do a kind act for anyone who asked a favor. James Heflin died September 16, 1892, at the age of forty-seven.

LUKE PRYOR BLACKBURN was born on June 16, 1816, in Woodford County, Kentucky. He received a medical degree from Transylvania University in 1835. He earned acclaim for establishing effective quarantines in the Mississippi River valley against yellow fever. He served the Confederacy in several ways, including an unsuccessful attempt to inflict Northern cities with yellow fever. He was charged with conspiracy to commit murder and did not return to Kentucky until 1872.[278]

His efforts during an 1878 yellow fever epidemic in Kentucky won him the appellation of "Hero of Hickman" and brought him the gubernatorial election victory. His work as governor focused on the single issue of prison reform. Recognizing the overcrowded prisons, Blackburn wrought his pardoning powers with haphazard regularity, pardoning more than one thousand people, which earned him the nickname "Lenient Luke." This action, amid increasing state violence, angered many. By the end of his four-year term, Blackburn had almost no allies. He was shouted down and booed by his own party. The press wrote about the pardon record of the man whom one paper called "the old imbecile."[279] Luke Blackburn died in 1887 at the age of seventy-one.

JOSEPH P. NUCKOLS was born on April 2, 1826, in Barren County, Kentucky. As a young man, he spent several years in California in search of his fortune. He returned to Kentucky, and as the Civil War broke out, he organized a company in Barren County, of which he was captain, and joined the Fourth Kentucky Infantry of the Confederate army. He had risen to the rank of colonel by the war's end. He was severely wounded a number of times. In 1876, he accepted the appointment of quartermaster and adjutant general of the state under Governor McCreary. He was reappointed adjutant general by Governor Blackburn and served until the close of Blackburn's term of office. Joseph P. Nuckols died on March 30, 1896, at the age of sixty-nine.

LABAN T. MOORE was born on January 13, 1829, in Wayne County, West Virginia, near Louisa, Kentucky. He graduated from Marietta College in Ohio and attended Transylvania Law College in Lexington, Kentucky. He commenced his law practice in Louisa. He was elected to the Thirty-Sixth Congress in 1859. During the Civil War, he established and enlisted in the Fourteenth Kentucky Infantry and was elected colonel in 1861. Afterward, he moved to Catlettsburg, Kentucky, and resumed practicing law. He served as a member of the Kentucky State Senate in 1881 and as a member of the Kentucky State Constitutional Convention in 1890 and 1891. He died in Catlettsburg in 1892 at the age of sixty-three.

PICTURES

Above: George Ellis hanged by a mob from a sycamore tree near the burned Gibbons house. *Public domain, courtesy of the Boyd County Public Library.*

Left: A rendering of the murder scene in the Gibbons house as told by George Ellis. *Public domain. Courtesy of the Boyd County Public Library.*

Pictures

A closer look at the hanged, George Ellis. *Public domain, courtesy of the Boyd County Public Library.*

Pictures

Grave markers of Fannie and Robbie Gibbons, buried in the historic Ashland Cemetery. *Author's collection.*

Left: Grave marker of Emma Carico in the historic Ashland Cemetery. *Author's collection.*

Right: Blackburn was the Kentucky governor who threatened to kill all of Boyd County to preserve the dignity of the law. *Courtesy of the National Library of Medicine.*

PICTURES

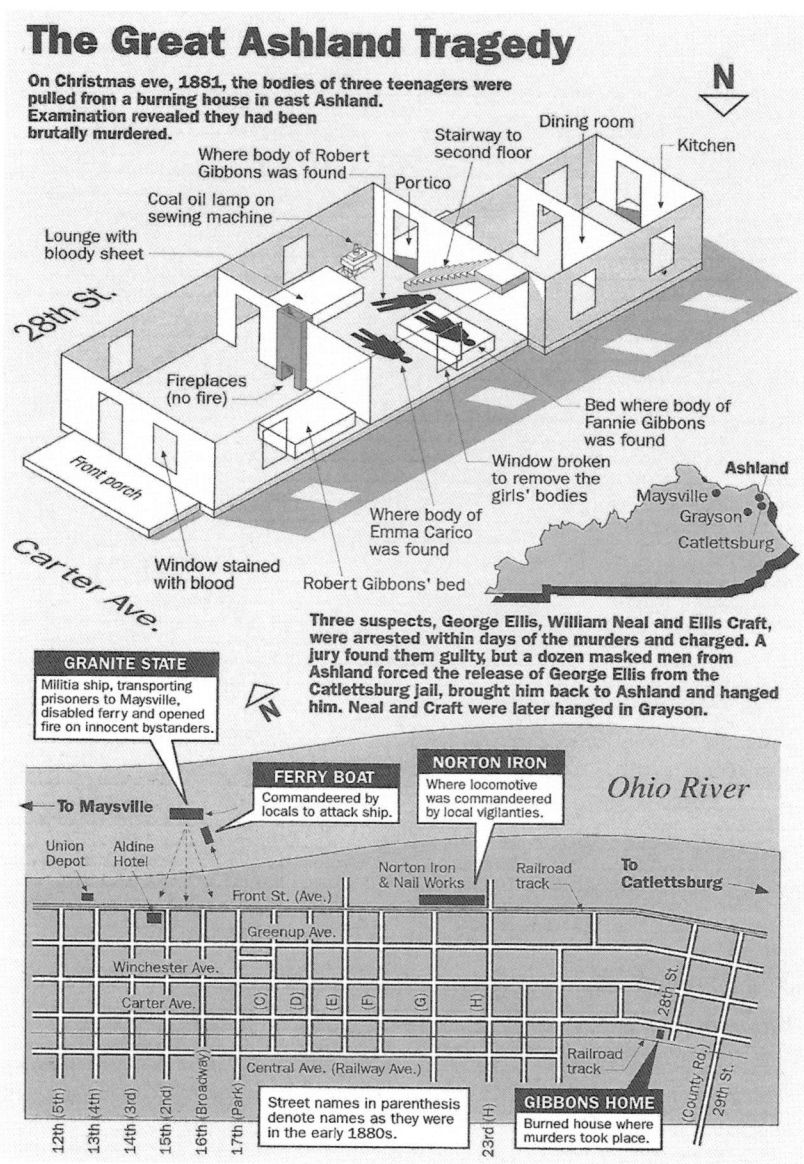

Courtesy of the Boyd County Library/Bill Martin.

NOTES

Preface

1. James M. Huff, *The Ashland Tragedy; The Crow-bar and the Ax—The Silent Witnesses* (Ashland, KY: J.M. Huff, circa 1885).
2. Ibid.

1. Introduction

3. *Courier-Journal* (Louisville, KY), October 13, 1883.
4. Ibid.
5. *Daily Independent* (Ashland, KY), October 25, 1883.
6. *Wheeling (WV) Register*, October 13, 1883.
7. *Cincinnati Enquirer*, June 13, 1883.
8. *Cincinnati Enquirer*, October 22, 1883.
9. *Cincinnati Enquirer*, January 12, 1882.
10. *Daily Independent*, October 25, 1883.
11. *Daily Independent*, October 18, 1883.
12. *Cincinnati Enquirer*, December 25, 1881.
13. *Atlanta Constitution*, December 29, 1881.
14. *Portsmouth (OH) Times*, January 7, 1882.
15. *Ironton (OH) Register*, Thursday, January 5, 1882.

16. John E. Kleber, *The Kentucky Encyclopedia* (Lexington: University Press of Kentucky, 1992), 36, 37.
17. Ibid.
18. *A History of Ashland, Kentucky 1786–1954* (Ashland, KY: Ashland Centennial Committee for the Celebration of its Centennial, Graber Printing Company), 4.
19. Ibid., 8.
20. Ibid., 22.
21. Ibid., 12.
22. Ibid., 9.

2. The Fire

23. *Daily Independent*, December 29, 1881.
24. Huff, *Ashland Tragedy*.
25. Ancestry.com. Martha Gibbons (née Rhodes) was born in 1835. John W. Gibbons was born in 1815, twenty years older than Martha.
26. *Cincinnati Enquirer*, December 17, 1881.
27. *Ironton Register*, December 30, 1881.
28. Huff, *Ashland Tragedy*.
29. Ancestry.com. Fannie Gibbons was born on November 22, 1867, making her barely fourteen years old. Emma Carico was born on December 28, 1867, making her four days shy of being fourteen years old.
30. Huff, *Ashland Tragedy*.

3. The Search

31. *Daily Independent*, December 29, 1881.
32. Huff, *Ashland Tragedy*.
33. *Daily Independent*, December 29, 1881.
34. Ibid.
35. *Highland Weekly News* (Hillsboro, OH), November 21, 1878.
36. George W. Atkinson and Alvaro F. Gibbens, *Prominent Men of West Virginia* (Wheeling, WV: W.L Callin, 1890), 914.
37. *Daily Independent*, December 29, 1881.
38. *Cincinnati Enquirer*, December 27, 1881.
39. *Cincinnati Enquirer*, December 26, 1881.

40. *Atlanta Constitution*, December 29, 1881.
41. *Cincinnati Enquirer*, December 27, 1881.
42. *Atlanta Constitution*, December 29, 1881.
43. *Cincinnati Enquirer*, December 27, 1881.
44. *Cincinnati Enquirer*, December 30, 1881.
45. Huff, *Ashland Tragedy*.
46. Ibid.
47. *Public Ledger* (Maysville, KY), September 16, 1892.
48. *New York Times*, March 13, 1881.
49. Ancestry.com. Emma L. Heflin was born on March 13, 1868, to James and Mary Heflin.
50. Huff, *Ashland Tragedy*.

4. Gibbons Found

51. *Daily Independent*, January 6, 1882.
52. Huff, *Ashland Tragedy*.
53. *Daily Independent*, January 6, 1882.
54. Ibid.
55. Ibid.
56. Ibid.
57. Ibid.
58. Huff, *Ashland Tragedy*.
59. *Daily Independent*, January 6, 1882.

5. A Confession

60. Huff, *Ashland Tragedy*.
61. Ibid.
62. Ibid.
63. Ibid.
64. *Courier-Journal*, February 10, 1882.
65. *Cincinnati Enquirer*, January 16, 1882.
66. *Courier-Journal*, January 6, 1882.
67. Huff, *Ashland Tragedy*.
68. Ibid.
69. *Courier-Journal*, January 4, 1862.

6. The River Chase

70. Huff, *Ashland Tragedy*.
71. Ibid.
72. Ibid.
73. Ibid.
74. *Cincinnati Enquirer*, January 6, 1882.
75. Kleber, *Kentucky Encyclopedia*.
76. Huff, *Ashland Tragedy*.
77. *Daily Independent*, January 12, 1882.
78. Ibid.
79. Ibid.
80. Huff, *Ashland Tragedy*.
81. Ibid.
82. Ibid.
83. *Courier-Journal*, January 7, 1882.
84. *Cincinnati Enquirer*, January 7, 1882.

7. Neal's Trial

85. *Cincinnati Enquirer*, January 10, 1882.
86. *Cincinnati Enquirer*, January 14, 1882.
87. Huff, *Ashland Tragedy*.
88. Ancestry.com. Thomas R. Brown was born on June 2, 1854, to Judge George and Sophia Brown.
89. Ancestry.com. Alexander Lackey was born on December 18, 1853, to Greenville and Rebecca Lackey.
90. *Biographical Encyclopedia of the Commonwealth of Kentucky* (1896), 112.
91. Ancestry.com. William C. Ireland was born November 18, 1823, to Samuel and Sarah Ireland.
92. *Cincinnati Enquirer*, January 18, 1882.
93. Ibid.
94. *Courier-Journal*, January 19, 1882.
95. Ibid.
96. Ibid.
97. *Courier-Journal*, January 21, 1882.
98. *Cincinnati Enquirer*, January 22, 1882.
99. Ibid.

100. *Courier-Journal*, January 22, 1882.
101. *Cincinnati Enquirer*, January 22, 1882.
102. *Courier-Journal*, January 22, 1882.
103. *Cincinnati Enquirer*, January 24, 1882.
104. *Daily Independent*, January 26, 1882.
105. *Cincinnati Enquirer*, January 24, 1882.
106. *Daily Independent*, January 26, 1882.
107. *Portsmouth Times*, January 21, 1882.
108. *Cincinnati Enquirer*, January 21, 1882.

8. Craft's Trial

109. Ancestry.com. The 1880 census lists Tilman Craft's occupation as grocer. In January 1884, a fire at his grocery store consumed his entire stock of goods, a valued loss of $3,000—per an article in the Wednesday, January 9, 1884 edition of the *Louisville Courier-Journal*.
110. *Daily Independent*, February 2, 1882.
111. Ibid.
112. *Cincinnati Enquirer*, January 27, 1882.
113. *Portsmouth Times*, January 28, 1882.
114. Huff, *Ashland Tragedy*.
115. Ibid.
116. Ibid.
117. *Portsmouth Times*, February 4, 1882.
118. *Daily Independent*, February 2, 1882.
119. Ibid.
120. Ibid.
121. Ibid.
122. *Cincinnati Enquirer*, February 8, 1882.
123. Huff, *Ashland Tragedy*.

9. Burnett's Theory

124. *Cincinnati Enquirer*, February 8, 1882.
125. Huff, *Ashland Tragedy*.
126. Ibid.
127. *Evening Bulletin* (Maysville, KY), February 9, 1882.

128. *Daily Independent*, February 23, 1882.
129. Huff, *Ashland Tragedy*.
130. Ibid.
131. *Cincinnati Enquirer*, February 15, 1882.
132. Atkinson and Gibbens, *Prominent Men*, 915.
133. *Cincinnati Enquirer*, February 14, 1882.
134. *Courier-Journal*, February 16, 1882.
135. *Cincinnati Enquirer*, February 24, 1882.
136. *Daily Independent*, March 2, 1882.
137. Ibid.
138. *Evening Bulletin*, February 16, 1882.
139. *Evening Bulletin*, April 14, 1882.
140. Huff, *Ashland Tragedy*.

10. George Ellis

141. Ibid
142. Ibid.
143. *Daily Independent*, June 8, 1882.
144. Ibid.
145. Ibid.
146. Huff, *Ashland Tragedy*.
147. Ibid.
148. *New York Times*, November 16, 1879.
149. *Evening Bulletin*, June 5, 1882.
150. *Evening Bulletin*, April 21, 1882.

11. New Trials

151. *Courier-Journal*, September 13, 1882.
152. *Courier-Journal*, November 5, 1882.
153. *Biographical Encyclopedia of the Commonwealth of Kentucky*, 240.
154. *Courier-Journal*, November 5, 1882.
155. Huff, *Ashland Tragedy*.
156. Ibid.
157. *Cincinnati Daily Gazette*, Thursday, November 2, 1882
158. Lowell H. Harrison and James C. Klotter, *A New History of Kentucky* (Lexington: University Press of Kentucky, 1997).

159. Edward Steers Jr., *Blood on the Moon: The Assassination of Abraham Lincoln* (Lexington: University Press of Kentucky, 2005). Luke Blackburn was arrested and tried for violating Canada's neutrality act. Though the evidence and public sentiment against him was overwhelming, he was acquitted by a Canadian court.
160. *Evening Bulletin*, November 2, 1882.
161 Huff, *Ashland Tragedy*.
162. *Courier-Journal*, November 9, 1882.
163. *Courier-Journal*, November 5, 1882.
164. Huff, *Ashland Tragedy*.

12. River Massacre

165. *Cincinnati Enquirer*, November 2, 1882.
166. Richard G. Stone Jr., *A Brittle Sword: The Kentucky Militia 1776–1912* (Lexington: University Press of Kentucky, 1978), 83.
167. Huff, *Ashland Tragedy*.
168. *Courier-Journal*, November 9, 1882.
169. *Daily Independent*, November 9, 1882; Ancestry.com. James McDonald was the husband of Florence Gibbons, eldest daughter of John and Martha Gibbons. He suffered multiple wounds from the firing soldiers at the river massacre and apparently died sometime later as a result of those wounds. At the 1900 census, Florence McDonald (née Gibbons) is listed as a widow.
170. Huff, *Ashland Tragedy*.
171. *Daily Independent*, November 9, 1882.
172. *Daily Independent*, November 23, 1882.
173. Stone, *Brittle Sword*, 84.
174. *Evening Bulletin*, November 3, 1882.
175. *Courier-Journal*, November 3, 1882. It was a common occurrence for people everywhere during that time period to congregate for the purpose of watching river traffic. It was considered a recreational pastime. There were no televisions, computers or video games that kept people fastened to the insides of their homes. And whenever a "special" boat passed by, large crowds of people would gather just to get a glimpse of it. For instance, when the Swedish soprano Jenny Lind left Louisville on the riverboat *Ben Franklin* on her way to Cincinnati in April 1851, large crowds of people gathered on the riverbanks at points in between just to get a glimpse of the boat.

176. *Cincinnati Enquirer*, April 24, 1851.
177. *Cincinnati Daily Enquirer*, March 12, 1879.
178. *Evening Bulletin*, November 7, 1882.
179. *Daily Independent*, November 9, 1882.
180. Stone, *Brittle Sword*, 85.
181. *Courier-Journal*, February 6, 1883.
182. Stone, *Brittle Sword*, 82.
183 Harrison and Klotter, *New History of Kentucky*, Kindle edition, loc. 2449.
184. Ibid., loc. 4643.
185. John David Preston, *The Civil War in the Big Sandy Valley of Kentucky* (Baltimore, MD: Gateway Press, 1984).
186. *Courier-Journal*, November 9, 1882.
187. *Wheeling Register*, November 3, 1882.
188. *Cincinnati Daily Gazette*, November 2, 1882.

13. Resolve and Recovery

189. *Courier-Journal*, November 10, 1882.
190. Huff, *Ashland Tragedy*.
191. *Cincinnati Daily Gazette*, November 2, 1882.
192. *Courier-Journal*, November 5, 1882.
193. Huff, *Ashland Tragedy*.
194. *Courier-Journal*, November 5, 1882.
195. Huff, *Ashland Tragedy*.
196. *Cincinnati Enquirer*, November 5, 1882.
197. *Daily Independent*, November 9, 1882.
198. Ibid.
199. *Daily Independent*, November 9, 1882; Ancestry.com. John Nist was the brother-in-law to Fannie and Robbie Gibbons. He was married to the second daughter of John and Martha Gibbons, Anna M. Gibbons.
200. John Calder was one of the three members of the Citizens Committee. He was a hardware merchant at the time of the murders and was elected Boyd County judge a few months later.
201. *Cincinnati Enquirer*, November 5, 1882.
202. Huff, *Ashland Tragedy*.
203. Ibid.

14. Ellis Craft

204. Ibid.
205. *Evening Bulletin*, November 14, 1882.
206. *Courier-Journal*, February 6, 1883.
207. *Evening Bulletin*, February 3. 1883.
208. *Courier-Journal*, February 6, 1883.
209. *Courier-Journal*, November 14, 1882. Private John M. Hurley was identified in some newspapers as Sergeant John M. Hierley and in others as Sergeant John M. Hurley. However, he was identified by Major Allen in his official report to the adjutant general as Private Hurley. It was Hurley's accidental shooting of himself that caused Major Allen to issue the order forbidding any private afterward to carry a pistol.
210. *Evening Bulletin*, November 15, 1882.
211. *Courier-Journal*, November 9, 1882.
212. *Courier-Journal*, February 6, 1883.
213. *Evening Bulletin*, February 8, 1883.
214. *Courier-Journal*, February 8, 1883.
215. *Cincinnati Enquirer*, February 15, 1883.
216. *Courier-Journal*, February 6, 1883.
217. *Cincinnati Enquirer*, February 15, 1883.
218. *Courier-Journal*, February 16, 1883.
219. *Courier-Journal*, February 18, 1883.
220. *Daily Independent*, March 1, 1883.
221. Ibid.
222. *Courier-Journal*, February 18, 1883.
223. *Cincinnati Enquirer*, February 24, 1883.
224. Ibid.
225. *Daily Independent*, March 1, 1883.
226. *Cincinnati Enquirer*, February 24, 1883.
227. *Daily Independent*, March 1, 1883.
228. Colonel Ernest MacPherson, *History of the First Regiment of Infantry—The Louisville Legion* (self-published, 1891).
229. *Evening Bulletin*, February 21, 1883.
230. *Courier-Journal*, February 21, 1883.
231. MacPherson *History of the First Regiment*.
232. *Courier-Journal*, March 3, 1883.
233. Harrison and Klotter, *New History of Kentucky*, loc. 3768.
234. Huff, *Ashland Tragedy*.

235. Ibid.
236. *Evening Bulletin*, June 18, 1883.
237. *Courier-Journal*, June 15, 1883.
238. *Courier-Journal*, June 20, 1883.
239. *Evening Bulletin*, June 19, 1883.
240. *Courier-Journal*, June 19, 1883.
241. *Evening Bulletin*, June 15, 1883.
242. *Evening Bulletin*, June 22, 1883.
243. *Evening Bulletin*, June 23, 1883.
244. *Breckinridge News* (Cloverport, KY), October 17, 1883.
245. Huff, *Ashland Tragedy*.
246. *Evening Bulletin*, June 13, 1883.
247. *Daily Independent*, October 18, 1883.
248. *Daily Independent*, June 7, 1883.
249. Ibid.
250. Ibid.
251. *Daily Independent*, March 1, 1883.
252. *Daily Independent*, June 14, 1883.
253. *Cincinnati Enquirer*, January 7, 1882.
254. *Wheeling Register*, October 13, 1883.
255. *Evening Bulletin*, October 15, 1883.
256. *Courier-Journal*, October 13, 1883.
257. *Hickman (KY) Courier*, October 19, 1883.
258. Ibid.
259. *Daily Independent*, October 18, 1883.

15. William Neal

260. *Courier-Journal*, April 26, 1884.
261. *Breckinridge News*, May 7, 1884.
262. Huff, *Ashland Tragedy*.
263. Ibid.
264. Huff, *Ashland Tragedy*.
265. *Hazel Green (KY) Herald*, April 1, 1885.
266. Huff, *Ashland Tragedy*.
267. Ibid.
268. Ibid.
269. *Evening Bulletin*, March 30, 1885.
270. *Evening Bulletin*, October 9, 1883.

16. Commentary

271. *Daily Independent*, October 18, 1883.
272. *Cincinnati Enquirer*, September 20, 1883.
273. *Daily Independent*, January 12, 1882.
274. *Courier-Journal*, November 9, 1882.
275. *Courier-Journal*, March 21, 1891.
276. *Evening Bulletin*, March 7, 1885.
277. *Owensboro (KY) Messenger*, October 19, 1883.

Brief Biographies

278. Judge Charles Kerr, *History of Kentucky*, vol. 2 (New York: American Historical Society, 1922).
279. Harrison and Klotter, *New History of Kentucky*.

ABOUT THE AUTHORS

JAMES MORGAN HUFF was born in Fleming County, Kentucky, on February 2, 1841. He was reared in Fleming County and learned blacksmithing under his father. He followed the trade about seventeen years and in 1872 removed to Ashland, where he was engaged in the mercantile business. In 1879, he relinquished the business and established a newspaper, the *Ashland Republican*. His six presses and six regular hands were necessary to meet his circulation of over 1,500, taking it to the front of journalism in Kentucky. As the Ashland Tragedy unfolded, beginning in December 1881, Huff chronicled much of the proceedings in a booklet titled *The Ashland Tragedy; The Crow-bar and the Ax—The Silent Witnesses*.

Huff witnessed several of the events during the time of the tragedy and was acquainted with many persons directly involved. His summarized account has been regarded as the most trusted of any summaries written about the tragedy until now. Huff was appointed secretary at the initial citizens meeting that met immediately following the crime. His writing was typical of the time, and his command of the English language permitted him to present authentic word pictures so his readers could visualize the actions as they took place. James Huff passed away on January 2, 1926, in Boyd County, Kentucky, at the age of eighty-four.

HERBERT E. "JOE" CASTLE was born in Ashland, Kentucky, and worked in that place for twenty-eight years. His bachelor's degree from Morehead State

About the Authors

University allowed him to focus his efforts on creative writing and history. His interest in the Ashland Tragedy was piqued after reading Huff's account several years prior to the printing of this book. He believed there was more to the story than what Huff had written. After years of extensive research, he found that to be true. Rather than re-write what Huff had already written, he felt it practical to preserve Huff's summarized account and augment it with the additional facts and details necessary to complete the history of this incredible true story.

Years of technical writing helped Castle become detail-oriented and create a welcoming writer-reader relationship giving the reader clear, precise and easy-to-understand language.

He has previously published a short story in the anthology series, *A Cup of Comfort for Fathers*, edited by Colleen Sell. Castle currently resides in Paintsville, Kentucky. He and his wife, Nancy, have three children and six grandchildren.

Visit us at
www.historypress.com